Joseph V
30/06/2018

The Rich Man Virus

Joseph Kabuleta

The Rich Man Virus

Copyright © 2015 **Joseph Kabuleta**

All rights reserved.

Publishing Consultion by

Evangel Publishing House,
Private Bag 28963 - 00200
NAIROBI. KENYA
info@evangelpublishing.org

ISBN 10: **9966-20-244-7**

ISBN 13: **978-9-966202-44-4**

Contents

Introduction v

Chapter 1
The rich man 1

Chapter 2
Characteristics of the rich man 13

Chapter 3
The deceitfulness of riches 47

Chapter 4
Easier for a camel 63

Chapter 5
Vaccination against the rich man virus 73

Chapter 6
Giving end or receiving end? 95

Chapter 7
Peddlers of the word 109

Introduction

For many years, Jesus' parable of Lazarus and the rich man intrigued me. It almost makes it seem like poor people like Lazarus have a fairer chance of going into Paradise and rich men are almost inexorably destined for eternal torment. This parable, as well as Jesus' statement that: "It's easier for a camel to go through the eye of a needle than for a rich man to enter the Kingdom of God", which is recorded in three gospel accounts, have been the basis of a religious mindset that treats wealth and those who possess it with deep suspicion.

The words of Jesus to the rich young ruler in Luke 18 to go and sell all he has, give the money to the poor and come and follow Him, were the basis of St Francis of Assisi's vow of poverty.

When Jesus spoke those words, the Bible says that His own disciples were greatly astonished. That's because the Jewish culture of the time fully believed, and with good reason, that wealth was a reward from God for obedience. From the Patriarchs Abraham, Isaac and Israel, to the Law, the Prophets, through to the time of the Gospels and the New Covenant, the word of God makes it clear that "God delights in the prosperity of his servants". So those words of the Lord appeared to be out of sync with the clear message of the Bible on the subject of wealth.

I sought to discover what Jesus really meant when he said it was easier for a camel to go through the eye of a needle than for 'a rich man' to enter the kingdom of God. None of the existing explanations satisfied my curiosity. I heard about the narrow gate in Jerusalem of old called 'the eye of a needle.' As far as this theory goes, camels that arrived after nightfall couldn't go through the main gate which would be locked at that time. The camels would be offloaded and would enter the city on their knees through the small 'eye of the needle' gate. This story has been the inspiration behind many tear-jerking sermons about coming without encumbrance on our knees to the Lord. It's all so compelling and touching but, sadly, untrue.

If that was true, then there would be no need for the disciples to be "greatly astonished" at those words, as the Bible says, or for them to wonder: "Who then can be saved?"

The 'eye of a needle' spoken of by Jesus is not symbolic, it is indeed the tiny hole in a seamstress' instrument.

However, Jesus' statement finally made sense when I discovered who the "rich man" of the Bible is; and it is not anybody who happens to be rich. You will learn in this book that the "rich man" refers to a peculiar type of personality with distinct traits outlined in this book. Then you will know that it is indeed "easier for a camel to go through the eye of a needle than for a "rich man" to enter the Kingdom of God.

Chapter 1

The rich man

At the peak of the world economic downturn in early 2009, at a time when businesses were being scythed down like ripe corn and people were losing their jobs and savings at an alarming rate, one particularly mulish banker in the United Kingdom was the subject of an impassioned debate that sucked in a whole nation.

It wasn't just about him; it was about a growing gulf between the bourgeoisie and proletariat, a disparity both in income and in perspective that was accentuated by this man's guts.

Sir Fred Goodwin was widely seen as being responsible for record losses at Royal Bank of Scotland. The bank was at the precipice after declaring a £24bn shortfall, easily the largest loss in UK Corporate history. The government shouldered a majority of the losses to keep the bank afloat, and that at a time when the average taxpayer was being pressed from every direction. The whole nation was understandably livid when it emerged that the man who had supervised over the record losses was making off with an annual pension of a million dollars or thereabout. The over-burdened taxpayers weren't just paying to clear up his mess, they were also giving the 50 year-old banker a lavish send-off that guaranteed a lifetime of comfort.

Public anger escalated to the point that Goodwin's house in Edinburgh was attacked by credit crunch protestors. The wave of rage extended to all those perceived to have been complicit in this apparent conspiracy. The minister responsible was under pressure to resign.

Yet, apparently, the government was powerless to slash any of Goodwin's £16m pension pot without breaching existing agreements. All they could do was cajole the world's worst banker, as the media called him, into voluntarily giving up part of his own contractual entitlement, if only to assuage public anger. But Goodwin was adamant.

Under intense pressure, the line minister wrote telling him that his refusal to reconsider was "unfortunate and unacceptable" and he hoped that "on reflection you will now share my clear view that the losses reported by the bank which you ran until October cannot justify such a huge reward".

As the debate raged on in the media and in government corridors, the man at the centre of it, as one tabloid reported, was holed away in a plush mansion in the south of France attending to golf and spa appointments in the company of his wife.

Surprisingly — or perhaps not — Goodwin, nicknamed

'The Shred' because of his ruthlessness in slashing thousands of jobs, perfected the role of a victim. As a whole nation flared up over this perceived injustice, Goodwin, through all his correspondences, cast himself as nothing but a convenient scapegoat for an economic crisis that couldn't entirely be his fault.

He insisted that he was "legally and morally" entitled to his full pension. In fact, in the words of another investment banker with whom he shared the same view, such a pension was "modest".

The most fascinating aspect of the debate wasn't so much the figures involved (which might seem big or small depending on the financial disposition of the reader) but the disparity in perspective.

At one end of the rift were enraged masses baying for blood. At the other end, the protagonist in chief and the few lucky who frolic with him were wondering what all the fuss was about.

One journalist captured the conflict so immaculately in *The Times* newspaper in the UK. Using her own experience, Minette Marrin described the unique world occupied by the rich man in a way that was so eye-catching. Here is an excerpt from her column.

"I first came across the filthy rich just after I was married and went to live in Hong Kong in the 1970s. Leaving poverty-stricken Britain, my husband and I joined a gold rush of bankers and brokers in what was then still a crown colony. What we saw was wealth and conspicuous consumption beyond the wildest dreams of avarice.

When I look back it seems like a dream – yachts and junks with boat boys, diamonds, gold, jade and bling, extravagant Chinese banquets, servants with bare feet and pigtails, pink and gold Mercedes, racing, gambling, water-skiing, jetting about and generally getting through loads of money because there was plenty more.

Though we weren't extremely highly paid, we spent a lot of time with people who were. Some were entrepreneurs and others were employees of banks and trading houses that, as today, offered them ways of making megabucks. Soon it became obvious **that being very rich is like catching an insidious virus.** Some people are able to resist it, but with most people the super-riches virus burrows into your nervous system for life. **It blurs your perspective, weakens your grasp on reality and changes your identity into someone who is entitled to be very rich.**

The rich man virus, as I call it, is not about property or bank balances. It is about an identity, about a sense of entitlement, about loss of perspective and ultimately about an intrinsic callousness towards the less privileged.

There is nothing quite like entitlement. It will make a person travel the world and do very daring things to get what they believe is theirs by right. It will make an obstinate banker stand up and fight for his million-dollar pension even if the whole nation sees it as a travesty.

From where he stood, Goodwin probably saw the public as ungrateful miscreants who didn't understand what wonderful things he had done for the banking sector. What might appear as greed or voraciousness to everyone else is all justified in the surreal context of entitlement.

While everybody else felt that Sir Fred Goodwin was being pointlessly stubborn in the face of such damning reality, he couldn't (not wouldn't) see it from their standpoint. That's an ability he had long lost. The ability to empathize with less privileged people is probably the first thing that walks out of the door when the rich man virus walks in.

So when he insisted that his million-dollar pension was modest, he was not bluffing. Far from it! He was being sincere, nearly as innocently sincere as Queen Marie-Antoinette when she (allegedly) said: "If they don't have bread let them eat cakes."

If they had been bluffing their statements wouldn't hold as much weight. But spoken, as it appears, from a position of sincerity, such remarks illustrate a loss of perspective that is the subject of this book.

The rich man virus and its ability to blur perspective is nothing new. It has existed through the ages. Here's one story from the Old Testament that illustrates the mindset of 'the rich man' and his skewed sense of entitlement.

"Then the LORD sent Nathan to David. And he came to him, and said to him: "There were two men in one city, one rich and the other poor.

The Rich Man Virus

*The rich man had exceedingly many flocks and herds. But the poor man had nothing, except one little ewe lamb which he had bought and nourished; and it grew up together with him and with his children. It ate of his own food and drank from his own cup and lay in his bosom; and it was like a daughter to him. And a traveler came to the **rich man**, who refused to take from his own flock and from his own herd to prepare one for the wayfaring man who had come to him; but he took the poor man's lamb and prepared it for the man who had come to him."* (2 Samuel 12:1-5)

From where you stand, the rich man from the above story is a heartless brute deserving of the strongest condemnation. King David certainly thought so. He even pronounced a quick death sentence for such merciless greed. But before you are tempted to get judgmental like David, spare a thought for the rich man.

He had so many sheep and like most wealthy men he wanted more. He had laid down foolproof strategies to ensure that he meets his target growth at the end of the year. Then one day he finds himself in a sticky situation. He must prepare one lamb for his visitor but it hurts to see his number diminish. He is already falling behind his target for the year and he should be moving forward not backward.

Then he gets an idea. There is this poor bloke next door who has a lamb but doesn't seem to understand its value. There's no chance he'll ever have more than just one. He has no ambition. He doesn't even need the lamb because it eats of his own food and a poor man has no food to waste.

This is all imaginative stuff, of course. None of it is spelt out in the Bible. But I am trying to show you the progression of thought that leads to a sense of entitlement and makes a rich man expect poor people to cheer when they are being deprived.

After a few minutes of brainstorming, the rich man is convinced that he is doing the poor man a favor by leaving him with one mouth less to feed. By the time he storms his neighbor's house to take the ewe, he feels completely justified.

The man behind the tale was King David himself, and yet he was the first person to pass a death sentence. Therein lays one of the foremost lessons you will pick from this book. The rich man virus is stealth in its operations and many people who are infected by it do not even realize that they have drifted off their values. That was true of David. It can creep into even the most well-meaning people and spread like a biological virus until it brings its host to ruin. Imagine David's shock when he learnt that the rapacious, merciless rich man of Nathan's parable was none other than himself.

One fine afternoon the king was strolling on the balcony of his palace when he saw a woman bathing in the neighborhood. He took a closer look and wow, wasn't she pretty? So the king went back to his palace with the picture implanted in his mind.

He inquired and learnt that she was married. That should have killed his interest but it didn't. He probably had a conversation with himself. 'I am the king and I can do as I please. In any case her husband is one of my junior officers and he is away in battle. So I will get away with it.'

The longer he thinks, the more attractive the idea seems.

By the time David sends for Bathsheba, he is probably convinced in his mind that he is entitled to having her anyway. After all, he is the king.

You can trust God to rebuke any of his servants whenever they start going down the rich man's path of illicit entitlement. The prophet Nathan showed up nearly as soon as the whole had episode played out.

In His judgment of David, delivered by Nathan, God said: *"I gave you your master's house and your master's wives into your keeping, and gave you the house of Israel and Judah. **And if that had been too little, I would also have given you more!**"* (2 Sam 12:8)

God made it clear that David could have gotten a lot more from Him without subverting the way justice. The rich man virus is not about what one has or doesn't have. It is not about property, bank balances or stock exchange listings, it's about an attitude. I have seen wealthy men who never catch the virus and I also know poor people who are severely afflicted by it. So if this book creates in you an aversion to wealth or those who possess it, you will sadly have missed my point.

Entitlement starts small and grows big. If God hadn't quickly called David to order, he would slowly but steadily have gone down the rebellious path of the kings of Israel and Judah that came after him.

One such king was Ahab, the husband of Jezebel. It's unusual for a king to be defined by his wife but this was a unique couple. Ahab had the fear of God, sort of. But he did a lot of evil because his wife drew him to it. Ahab was initially suffering from a mild version of the rich man virus but he let it grow until it eventually led to his premature death.

*"And it came to pass after these things that Naboth the Jezreelite had a vineyard which was in Jezreel, next to the palace of Ahab king of Samaria. So Ahab spoke to Naboth, saying, "**Give me your vineyard, that***

I may have it for a vegetable garden, *because it is near, next to my house; and for it I will give you a vineyard better than it. Or, if it seems good to you, I will give you its worth in money." (1* Kings 21:1-6)

But Naboth said to Ahab, "The LORD forbid that I should give the inheritance of my fathers to you!"

Consider the denigrating nature of Ahab's proposal. What the king was asking for was a treasured piece of property for Naboth, with both material and sentimental value. That's why he had a vineyard on it. Then along comes someone richer and more powerful (in the contemporary world those two go together) who wanted to annex his ancestral property to use it for a vegetable garden (!) I would think a vineyard is a nobler use for treasured piece of land than a vegetable garden. So not only did King Ahab want to annex his land, he wanted to put it to less honorable use. It's like your rich neighbor asking to buy your family house so he can raze it and expand his parking lot? It's no wonder Naboth was outright in his refusal. And Ahab's reaction spoke volumes.

So Ahab went into his house sullen and displeased because of the word which Naboth the Jezreelite had spoken to him; for he had said, "I will not give you the inheritance of my fathers." And he lay down on his bed, and turned away his face, and would eat no food.

When a king who is so wealthy he lives in an ivory house (1 Kings 22:39) loses his sleep over an extra piece of land he cannot have, it is clear he has developed a sense of entitlement. He is becoming the rich man. But he wasn't yet terminally afflicted. He still had the fear of God in him so he wouldn't take the vineyard forcefully even if, as king, he could.

But Jezebel his wife came to him, and said to him, "Why is your spirit so sullen that you eat no food?"

He said to her, "Because I spoke to Naboth the Jezreelite, and said to him, 'Give me your vineyard for money; or else, if it pleases you, I will give you another vineyard for it.' And he answered, 'I will not give you my vineyard.'"

Then Jezebel his wife said to him, "You now exercise authority over Israel!..."

She went ahead to arrange the death of Naboth and delivered the vineyard to her husband who gleefully possessed it. You would think that Ahab would be satisfied after he got the property over which he had lost several nights of sleep. But that's not how the rich man virus operates. The vineyard only served to whet his appetite. His penchant for forceful possession grew bigger until he felt entitled to cities that didn't belong to him.

And the king of Israel (Ahab) said to his servants, "Do you know that Ramoth in Gilead is ours, but we hesitate to take it out of the hand of the king of Syria?" (2 Kings 22:3)

And so Ahab joined with Jehoshaphat king of Judah and readied himself for war over Ramoth in Gilead. Even if his mind was made up, he assembled 400 prophets to put up a show of inquiring from the Lord. They all told him what he wanted to hear.

Yet they sent for another prophet, Micaiah, whom Ahab confessed to hate "because he does not prophesy good concerning me, but evil" (in other words, he doesn't prophesy what I want to hear like all the rest but speaks the true oracles of God).

Ahab knew from his conscience that he wasn't supposed to go to war, because even when Micaiah initially joined in the chorus of the other prophets and promised victory over Syria, the king was not convinced.

"How many times shall I make you swear that you tell me nothing but the truth in the name of the LORD?" Ahab replied.

And so prophet Micaiah was emboldened and spoke the true word from God foretelling Ahab's death in battle. But the king was already bubbling with greed and a false sense of entitlement. He wasn't going to be deterred from his chosen course of action. So he gave instructions that: *"Put this fellow (the prophet) in prison, and feed him with bread of affliction and water of affliction, until I come in peace."*

Of course Ahab didn't return in peace. The rich man virus and its principal symptoms that are greed and entitlement put a hook in his nose and led him to his death. To this day, the rich man virus is still in the business of leading people to their death; physical as well as spiritual.

In fact, you will be shocked to learn what the Bible has to say about the rich man, then you will understand what Jesus meant when he said *"it's easier for a camel to go through the eye of a needle than for a rich man to enter the kingdom of God."*

Chapter 2

Characteristics of the rich man

F or a number of years running up to 2009, at a time when I worked as a journalist and columnist for a leading newspaper in Uganda, I frequently met a number of extremely wealthy people by the standards of my country.

I got to know most of them through their involvement in football and I got to meet several others through those I met in sport. Even if I didn't know it at the time, I believe God arranged those meetings for the purpose of the message that I share in this book. Through those encounters I got to know how rich men think. It's markedly different from the way other people think; and by other people I do not mean poor people.

When you come to understand, hopefully through this book, how the rich man thinks, you will fully understand what

Jesus meant when He said: *"It's easier for a camel to go through the eye of a needle than for a rich man to enter the Kingdom of God."*

You will know for sure that the 'eye of a needle' the Lord was referring to is not a narrow gate into old time Jerusalem (like some people preach) but the tiny opening in a seamstress's instrument.

My leisurely meetings with those tycoons were often on Sunday afternoons over several cups of coffee. We talked about everything; football, family but mostly about their wealth. Even though we were worlds apart in income, they seemed to enjoy my company and never once slighted me. I found that to be remarkable.

Still, I couldn't help but notice that most of them were prickly and sensitive. But they covered up their insecurity with the kind of superficiality that would seem silly or even juvenile to people in the lower financial stratum characterized by careers, salaries, mortgages; the world in which I existed. These rich men never seemed to allow conversations to veer far off their darling subject of wealth; how they made it, what lovely places they have visited spending it and how much more they have than seems apparent. I was supposed to be impressed and for spells I acted impressed, even blown away. I know this might sound a bit like sour grapes but I remember thinking to myself that, given the chance, I wouldn't exchange my life for theirs.

Many of them have such a jaundiced attitude to life that measures their happiness not just by what comes to them, but also by what doesn't go to their rivals, both real and perceived. It's a world of cutthroat competition in which success is relative to what's happening next door. I don't want to be in a position where I can have everything I want and still be miserable because people I consider to be competition have just as much, or more.

These men were always nice to me because I made for good audience. I was just a journalist on a modest salary who never threatened the exclusivity of their club. But the same men would suddenly become odious when talking about other rich people whom they considered to be rivals.

It's a characteristic I see in many top sportsmen too. Tiger Woods and Phil Mickelson were once reported to be good friends. That was when one of them was winning almost all the golf majors and the other was simply getting along. But the 'friendship' fell apart the moment Mickelson started winning some majors of his own. Before long the animosity between them was undisguised. It's easy for a top sportsman to be cordial with a fellow professional who is not in his class. But even the most apparently good-natured stars become spiteful the moment their position is threatened. I am building upon a point that will become clearer as we go along.

Here are some characteristics that define the rich man.

a) Their wealth is their identity

The rich man's wealth is his strong city, And like a high wall in his own esteem. (2 Samuel 12:1-5)

My time with rich men taught me that, for most of them, their wealth had become their identity. They couldn't see themselves besides their vast estates. Their only sense of worth was their stock exchange worth.

Anybody who defines himself by what he owns has built his life on a very rickety foundation. Companies collapse, sometimes for no apparent reason. Jobs and careers end too, and the people who built their lives around them are left empty, struggling for a reason to live.

Losing a company or a job hurts for everyone. But it hurts much more for those who haven't just lost a source of income but have lost their identity too.

Some of them are tempted to take the plunge.

Some do.

Many did during the 2008/09 credit crunch.

One of them was German billionaire Adolf Merckle.

Shortly before 5pm one Monday in January 2009, the 74-year-old put on his coat, told his wife "I have to go to the office for a while". He drove to a railway embankment near his home, where he lay on the frozen tracks and waited patiently for his death. It wasn't long before a speeding train came and took him out of his misery.

Once ranked the 94th richest man in the world by Forbes magazine, the industrialist had seen his wealth ebbing away as the global recession took hold, leaving him, in the words of his family, a broken man. So many theories on the possible breaking point were explored in the media — his suicide note said simply: "I am sorry" — but the words of his long-time friend offered the best explanation.

"His companies were his life. When he was going to lose control of them he obviously felt he would lose control of his life."

"Mr Merckle is not the first high-profile figure to commit suicide during the financial crisis," one newspaper wrote in January 2009. "Just before Christmas, fund manager Thierry de la Villehuchet, who had invested with the alleged fraudster Bernard Madoff, was found dead in his New York office after taking sleeping pills and slashing his wrists. Barry Fox, a Bear Stearns analyst, jumped from his 29th-floor office last year after losing his job."

The newspaper concluded: "The sad truth is that there will almost certainly be others as the recession bites deeper. But those who are left behind will never fully comprehend how pride and prestige can ever be more valuable than life itself."

But that's precisely what happens when a clear line is not drawn between the person and the purse.

There are many rich people, however, who successfully detach themselves from their possessions in a way that either one can exist without the other. I know one such man in my country. One newspaper went about asking rich people the same question: "What's the secret of your success."

The modest ones put it down to a lucky break in business that set them on their way but a majority of them exuded pomp, attributing their wealth to rare qualities, virtues or insight that they only possess. It made for splendid reading. It's amazing how much you can learn about a person by asking such a simple question.

But this particular man replied curtly: "I do not consider myself to be successful."

The reporter asked no further questions.

He should have.

I did, when I met him at a restaurant.

"I will consider myself successful when I have raised all my children into responsible adults," he said. For a moment I thought he was trying to sound smart, until I heard the full story. This man has put his children through a sort of training program that is so rigorous it borders on cruelty. "If they aren't given a proper training," he said, "the wealth that is meant to help them will destroy them."

That's hardly all. He is avuncular and has extended a helping hand to many upcoming businessmen in town. Unlike most of the others I used to meet, here is one wealthy man who seems to have kind and even helpful words for people trying to break into his bracket. Our conversation inevitably switched to another formerly rich man who had only recently lost his entire estate to creditor banks. While most other rich men I knew were celebrating their rivals' downfall, this man was truly saddened by his plight.

He is rich. But he is not the rich man.

b) Lifetime pursuit

For no sooner has the sun risen with a burning heat than it withers the grass; its flower falls, and its beautiful appearance perishes. So the rich man also will fade away in his pursuits. (James 1:11)

Everyone wants to be rich. Well, at least most people do. God definitely wants His children to be rich. Paul says in 2Corinthians 6:10 that his teaching was *"making many rich"*. So prosperity preachers, as they are often and sometimes derisively called, aren't just a modern day phenomenon. Paul was the first prosperity preacher.

For you know the grace of our Lord Jesus Christ, that, though he was rich, yet for your sakes he became poor, that you through his poverty might be rich. (2 Cor 8:9)

However, the Bible warns of 'the love of money' which is stated as 'the root of all evil.' That scripture, along with the camel and the eye of the needle, have been the subject of so many skewed, mostly religious interpretations which use them to demonize wealth and those who possess it or preach about it.

But Paul, just a few verses down the same chapter, says that God gives us riches to enjoy. The Amplified translation says *"God, Who richly and ceaselessly provides us with everything for [our] enjoyment."* (1 Tim 6:17)

So the big question is; at what stage does a normal desire for wealth and the enjoyment of it (a good thing) turn into the love of money (a bad thing)?

From the outside, it's a fine line that separates the two positions. But inside the heart of the protagonist, it's a whole paradigm shift.

The love of money is a mindset that places wealth above every other consideration and turns a person's life into an endless pursuit of it. It is, in the language of this book, catching the rich man virus. Just like someone who catches the HIV virus doesn't change outwardly in the short run, someone who has crossed the line into the love of money similarly looks unchanged to the outside observer. He works just like before, balances the same books, preaches the same messages, with as much fervor as before, attends to the same needs and so on. But inwardly, everything has changed, starting with his priorities.

Just like the HIV virus, the rich man virus often takes its time silently eating away at its victim but eventually — and it can take several years — outside observers start to notice a difference. When the HIV virus is through with its work, its host is dead. When the rich man virus has completed its work, it turns its host into a slave of mammon; spiritually dead.

Money is a good servant but a terrible master. When it gains the ascendency in a man's heart it becomes an end in itself rather than a means to an end. To the rest of us, money is a means to a better life for ourselves and for the people around us. But for the rich man, wealth is accumulated for the sheer joy of having it. He cannot have enough of it. He craves for more. He lives for the new figures. The Bible says that: *"...those who crave to be rich fall into temptation and a snare and into many foolish (useless, godless) and hurtful desires that plunge men into ruin and destruction and miserable perishing."* (1 Tim 6:9 AMP)

In the same way that a junkie will justify larceny to satisfy a craving, the rich man will rationalize all things in his relentless pursuit of the next million.

In its extreme stages, the rich man virus indisposes its victim of any sensitivity or affection and turns him into a money-making automaton. That is its ultimate purpose.

The wise man of Ecclesiastes states that: *"He who loves silver will not be satisfied with silver; Nor he who loves abundance, with increase. This is vanity."* (Ecc 5:10)

You are probably already shocked at how many times the

Bible refers to the rich man, and how by that it does not mean any man who happens to be rich. If you have already made a distinction between the two, then you now know what Jesus meant when he said *"it is easier for a camel to go through the eye of a needle than for a rich man to enter the Kingdom of God."*

The futility of a lifetime pursuit of wealth

Proverbs 1:16-18:

Surely, in vain the net is spread
In the sight of any bird;
But they lie in wait for their own blood,
They lurk secretly for their own lives.
So are the ways of everyone who is greedy for gain;
It takes away the life of its owners.

In all likelihood, the rich man never realizes the futility of his life until it's coming to an end.

Only then does his perspective return ever so briefly. Then he suddenly realizes that he was too busy chasing after wealth to spare any time to enjoy it. If he is honest with himself, and we usually are in the face of death, he will realize that he has been dead for many years. He died the day he lost his sensitivity, warmth, affection and all those tender virtues that make us human; he died the day he exchanged his soul for figures and more figures, the moment he started seeing everyone through the prism of his money.

Proverbs 15:27: *He who is greedy for gain troubles his own house...*

While still on the death bed, he realizes that he didn't just lose himself. He probably lost his family too at the time in his life when he became too busy to cultivate meaningful relationships. He looks back to the day when people ceased to be delicate beings deserving of love and became labor; just another factor of production.

Surely every man walks about like a shadow; Surely they busy themselves in vain; He heaps up riches, And does not know who will gather them. (Psalms 39:6)

So he looks into the faces of the people around his sickbed; his wife, if he still has any, possibly former wives too, his children, grand children and other relatives whom he cannot place. None of them looks particularly grief-stricken. He cannot blame them. He has been a stranger to them for so many years. He was never a part of their lives. Many of them are standing at his bedside out of obligation. They can scarcely disguise the fact that they would rather be elsewhere. They are probably all wondering what is in his will. They cannot wait for him to die so they can find out who takes what. They are anxious to devour what he spent a lifetime gathering. The futility of his money-chasing life is realized before his own eyes.

Am I being cynical in painting a grim ending to a rich man's life? Hardly!

The Bible paints a similarly inglorious conclusion to the life of people who spend their days in an obsessive hunt for riches.

*"There is one alone, without companion: He has neither son nor brother. Yet there is no end to all his labors, nor is his eye satisfied with riches. But he never asks, "For whom do I toil and deprive myself of good?" This also is vanity and **a grave misfortune.**"* (Ecclesiastes 4:8)

It's interesting that a fortune can become 'a grave misfortune' in the end.

The scripture says that "he never asks…"

He never stops to ask himself 'why and for whom am I doing all this?'

The family and loved ones who should be the beneficiaries have probably long been estranged. Faced with such a dilemma, and after deep moments of introspection, most people have opted to bequeath all their wealth to charity or some other noble cause. It's usually a last ditch attempt to reconnect with their conscience, or the part of it that they subdued when their heart switched to money.

c) Not generous

"There was a certain rich man who was clothed in purple and fine linen and fared sumptuously every day. But there was a certain beggar named Lazarus, full of sores, who was laid at his gate, desiring to be fed with the crumbs which fell from the rich man's table. Moreover the dogs came and licked his sores. So it was that the beggar died, and was carried by the angels to Abraham's bosom. The rich man also died and was buried. And being in torment in Hades, he lifted up his eyes and saw Abraham afar off, and Lazarus in his bosom. (Luke 16:19-23)

If you do not understand what the Bible means by the rich man — how that refers to a peculiar identity and not just the possession of wealth — you could be led to believe that Jesus was advocating for poverty. The story of Lazarus and the rich man in particular makes it look like all affluent people are headed for torment while poor folks have a fairer chance of spending their life hereafter in a place of comfort which was called Abraham's bosom. But if that was the case, Abraham himself wouldn't be there because he lived his earthly life in luxury. He wasn't just rich; the Bible says he was very rich in livestock, in silver and in gold.

But when you study the passage carefully you will notice that the rich man of that parable wasn't just rich, he was the rich man.

And it's worth noting that every time the Bible speaks of the rich man (one afflicted with the rich man virus), he is never mentioned by name. Jesus could have said that there was a rich man and a poor man. But He went ahead to tell us that the poor man was called Lazarus. But the rich man was just that; the rich man. That's a clear indication that their wealth has become their identity.

The passage states that Lazarus desired to feed on the rich man's leftovers. The word 'desire' paints a picture of deprivation. The NIV Bible translation uses the word 'longing'. He wouldn't desire or long for the crumbs if he always got them. Therefore the parable is about a man so callous he wouldn't let the beggar sitting at his gate have his leftovers.

That lack of sympathy or empathy towards those in need is one of the foremost signs of the rich man virus. It's something every believer must be on the look-out for. The day you catch yourself sneering at that 'irritant' trying to catch your attention to ask for small change, you should stop and examine yourself. I am not suggesting that you feel obligated to give something to every beggar that stands in your face. What you should check constantly is your attitude towards the less privileged. Does it tend towards empathy or irritation?

The rich man virus, like a biological virus, does not announce its entry. All that you will ever see is its devastation, and that often comes when it is too late for most people to reverse the trend.

The rich man attitude can creep into even the most well-meaning people and cause them to justify their hostility towards the poor. I am sure the rich man in Jesus' parable had a perfectly logical argument for denying Lazarus the leftovers from his sumptuous meals.

"The trouble with these beggars is that once you give him food it becomes your responsibility to feed him," the rich man would tell his friends over a cup of coffee on the balcony of his mansion, as the leftovers from their sumptuous are fed to the dogs.

"Before I know it, scores of beggars will be sitting outside my gate, littering my lawns and expecting me to feed them too.

"The next thing I will be feeding the whole town."

"The government should do something about these people before they become a nuisance on our streets," one of his friends suggests.

"Indeed it should," the rich man continues, "we pay a lot in taxes and we deserve a clean neighborhood free of these parasites."

Of course that conversation is from my imagination. It's aimed at showing you how, over the course of a few minutes of conversation, heartlessness can be justified, permitted then preferred, in that order. That's what the rich man virus does. And the people who catch it do not realize that it is eating away at their heart little by little. Before they know it, *it's easier for a camel to go through the eye of a needle*......

The contemporary world has come up with an innovative way of making people who aren't necessarily generous look generous. It's called charity. Big charity organizations have mustered the art of cajoling their donors into signing the next big check at high-end cocktails in the public glare where it's all done for the show. It's a system that appeals to the donor's ego rather than his or her heart. Consequently, it creates benefactors and philanthropists but not necessarily generous people; at least not in the Biblical sense. True godly generosity springs from the heart and from compassion towards those in need.

The rich man of Jesus' story might have woken up one morning, walked past Lazarus, looked briefly at the dogs licking his wounds and looked the other way in disgust, then drove into town to give a big donation to charity when the setting was right; amid media cameras and other rich people whom he wants to impress. I am just imagining what scenarios could have played out in the modern world.

I guess you could argue that the end justifies the means. Rich men donate money to charity and people in need are helped; which is a wonderful thing. But you can never separate God from motives.

d) Entitled to more

It would have been the largest single charitable donation in Panama's history, but it never was. It never was going to be.

An American tycoon called Wilson Lucom, who died in 2006 aged 88, made a will that stunned not just Panama, but the world and, especially, his own family. It granted his wife a monthly stipend of $20,000 and gave her children one-off payments ranging from $50,000 to $200,000. But the big prize – an estate whose value was more than $50m – was to be sold off and the proceeds given to a newly-created foundation for poor children in Panama.

Lucom's old and ailing widow Hilda, an octogenarian matriarch of the Arias family, comes from one of the most powerful dynasties in Panama which has extensive media, property and financial interests. Her five children from a previous marriage (Lucom had no children of his own) are scions of a family which boasts former presidents, ministers and diplomats.

They are the sort of people you would think didn't need the money. But that doesn't mean they didn't want it. In fact, they wanted it badly enough to challenge the validity of the will, claiming that Lucom had been manipulated by his advisers.

The lawyer representing the poor children, a long time friend of Lucom, came under intense attack. He was charged with 15 criminal charges including negligent homicide in Lucom's death, forgery, extortion and perfidy. He was placed on an Interpol list. He claimed it was a smear campaign. "It's amazing what they did to me," he lamented.

Several lower courts in Panama upheld the will as reflecting Lucom's last wishes but the rich family of his wife took it higher and higher up the judicial ladder until, after four years of litigation involving 20 legal firms, Panama's supreme court declared the will void in October 2010, arguing that Lucom's reference to his "beloved wife" showed he really wanted her, and not poor children, to inherit the estate.

"I'm sad and disgusted," bemoaned the lawyer representing the children. "It's a joke. They stole that money, it's that simple. Kids are starving and a few (rich) individuals have walked away with everything."

Naturally, critics abounded. They accused the tycoon's widow of greed and questioned the integrity of Panama's judicial system. "That money could have helped a lot of children. If that family keeps it God will not forgive them," said Hector Avila, head of a children's charity. "In this country political and economic forces weigh more than justice."

Despite Panama's relatively high-income per capita (US$13,595 in 2011) poverty remains pervasive, according to a World Bank report. That is because most of the country's wealth is concentrated among a few. Over one million people (37 percent of the population) live below the poverty line. Of these, over half a million (19 percent) live in extreme poverty. One-half of all Panamanian children are poor. All of them stood to benefit from the American tycoon's generosity.

But his widow wasn't just fighting for herself. She was fighting for an aristocracy; for a system which believes that wealth should stay among the wealthy.

That's what the rich man virus does. It births in its victims a belief that they have the right to be rich and richer; and poor people should be comfortable with their station in life. It's not unlike the old Roman system where lords and nobles were entitled to wealth and honor and they expected common people not just to be contented with their lowly place, but also to work hard to maintain the status quo. It was a system of inherent inequality rooted in and sustained by the culture of the time.

These days there is another similar social classification arrangement based on wealth. Even if the people at the bottom end aren't necessarily acquiescent (actually they actively fight it) those at the top believe they have every right to be there; and they fully expect the less privileged to meekly comply.

The rich man hates to see money go into the hands of the poor. He believes they have no use for it. I often heard rich men ask about poor people who had gotten a sudden windfall, may be through the lottery or some other means: "What's he going to do with all that money?"

There's a lot more to that question than plain curiosity. In fact, their tone is often so pejorative it wouldn't be different if they were asking what a dog is going to do with a gold necklace.

There's a friend of mine who, out of his generous nature, decided to pay his nanny a salary that is way above the going rate. He believes that someone who looks after his daughters should be happy in her job. But there's a neighbor of his who is deeply bothered by such wanton magnanimity.

"You are the one spoiling these ladies," the neighbor often complains. "That is a lot of money for her. She doesn't need it."

That neighbor may not be rich, but he is definitely a rich man.

The rich man is convinced that money is an unnecessary burden for poor people because they are happier without it. Why rattle their simple, torpid existence with a lot of money?

The rich man is convinced that money is better off in the hands of people who have loads of it. They are the ones who know its value. Why give a kid a million when you can give it a sweet?

It's important to understand that the rich man doesn't believe he is doing anything wrong by depriving the poor. On the contrary, he believes that a poor man's cry for justice — like the case of Lucom's $50m estate — is not unlike a kid kicking and screaming because his parents have taken a unique toy out of his hand, which toy happens to be a loaded gun. The kid or the poor man is only upset because they don't know that it's for their own good.

That sense of entitlement — and complete change of perspective — is the single biggest symptom of the rich man virus and it's what gives birth to the next symptom.

e) Defrauds his workers of their wages

"Come now, you rich, weep and howl for your miseries that are coming upon you. (James 5:1-4)

Your riches are corrupted, and your garments are moth-eaten. Your gold and silver are corroded, and their corrosion will be a witness against you and will eat your flesh like fire. You have heaped up treasure in the last days. **Indeed the wages of the laborers who mowed your fields, which you kept back by fraud, cry out;** *and the cries of the reapers have reached the ears of the Lord of Sabaoth.*"

I got an early introduction to the routine fleecing of workers that characterizes the rich man's world at my first paid job which I took in-between academic years at college. The root of such fraud is entitlement, which gives birth to impunity and makes rich men feel like they can do as they please with the hard-earned wages of their employees.

I was working at a construction site for a company which was building a plush home for a rich and politically-connected man on one of the hills overlooking Kampala. I often worked up to dusk because I was paid by the day and my immediate supervisors had to wring every last minute from me. I remember trudging home every evening, too exhausted to even catch a minute of television, but happy that I was earning for the first time in my life.

One afternoon two lads came around the work place, almost of similar age; I would say in their early 30s. They stayed a few hours until the wealthy man who owned the building passed by late in the evening. He stepped out of his Cross Country Mercedes and had a small chat with them. They agreed on a fee to plaster the massive living room, dining, and study.

The lads were at the work place before I got there the following morning. They formed such an effective partnership and earned a living as plastering experts. One of them would apply the first coat of mortar while the other followed behind doing the smoothening. Then the first one would return and apply the finishing touch. They had done that sort of thing for years and could work at a supersonic speed without compromising the quality. Before sunset that very day, they were done. We were in shock.

And so was the owner. When he pulled his massive frame out of the wagon that evening, the two lads approached him and announced that the work was done. But instead of paying them, he flared up. He expected the work to be done in a week or so and had negotiated the pay accordingly. But there it was, neatly done in a day. He paced up and down the rooms, closely inspecting the walls, but failed to find fault.

He felt cheated. He tried to re-negotiate downwards so he could pay the lads something closer to a day's wages but they were smarter than that. They insisted on their full remuneration. In the end, he gave them nothing. Not a cent.

After a couple of weeks passing by every evening, all hope for getting paid faded and they gave up. It's not like the owner didn't have the money. But he kept it back just because he could.

I couldn't believe his impunity. It was like taking a sweet from a child.

Jeremiah 22:13: *"Woe to him who builds his house by unrighteousness*

And his chambers by injustice, Who uses his neighbor's service without wages

And gives him nothing for his work,

Of course I am now more accustomed to such injustice. But I have also come to know a Judge who shows no partiality, who cannot be unduly influenced; a Judge who can be approached by any justice-seeker without the need for lawyers and legal fees. He's name is Jehovah.

Psalms 35: 10: *"All my bones shall say, "LORD, who is like You,*

Delivering the poor from him who is too strong for him,

Yes, the poor and the needy from him who plunders him?""

My brother Edgar was once fleeced of what was (to him at the time) a princely sum of money. He had paid a rich man in town to deliver a product which was never delivered. Yet the man had no intentions of making a refund. It turned out the man was a notorious crook, but my brother hadn't known about his infamy at the time of their dealing.

So everywhere he went to lodge a complaint they simply laughed at him.

"If you were stupid enough to pay him upfront then you have yourself to blame," he was roundly told. Edgar initially considered taking the loss manfully and moving on but later decided to take his case to the highest court. While in prayer, God told him to ignore the man and address the spirit using that man to defraud him. And so he did.

Weeks went by and nothing happened. Then one day the man called my brother and asked him over to his shop. He sounded like he was in panic. He was seated behind the counter, enraged but scared. His wife counted out the money and Edgar left with the full refund. Up to this day my brother wonders what the man saw that scared him out of his wits, but it must be the only time that man ever refunded anybody.

In much of the developed world, such injustice is curtailed by strong corporate structures, labor laws and trade unions. But the world which I inhabit brings out this rich man weakness in its rawest form. The absence of such structures coupled with high unemployment leaves workers at the mercy of their employers. In such a loose system, only the most skilled workers who cannot easily be replaced get their due in wages and only the most honorable employers deal faithfully with their employees. Left to their own devices, many employers behave like the man I call the godfather of capitalist greed.

Centuries before the word was even coined, Laban in the book of Genesis exhibited all the characteristics of a modern day capitalist. This discourse from Jacob tells the full story of what is was like working for Laban.

"These twenty years I have been with you; your ewes and your female goats have not miscarried their young, and I have not eaten the rams of your flock.

That which was torn by beasts I did not bring to you; I bore the loss of it. You required it from my hand, whether stolen by day or stolen by night. There I was! In the day the drought consumed me, and the frost by night, and my sleep departed from my eyes.

Thus I have been in your house twenty years; I served you fourteen years for your two daughters, and six years for your flock, and you have changed my wages ten times.

Unless the God of my father, the God of Abraham and the Fear of Isaac, had been with me, surely now you would have sent me away empty-handed. God has seen my affliction and the labor of my hands, and rebuked you last night." (Genesis 31:38-42)

After Jacob had worked seven years for Rachel, he was given Leah, the elder sister, and told to work another seven years for the woman he loved. A true capitalist knows what his employees crave for and will almost definitely use it against them. You could call them incentives; those attractive packages which employers dangle in front of their best employees to prolong their period of servitude, just like Laban did with Jacob. And seven years seemed like a few days for Jacob because he loved Rachel that much.

That begs the question: Is there any incentive that would make seven years seem like a few days for you? Is it really worth seven years of toil or is someone exploiting you?

A true capitalist seeks to squeeze every drop of service from the best of his employees and will gladly let them go away empty handed when they have nothing left to offer.

Laban the capitalist knew that God had blessed his herd because of Jacob, and he loved him for that. But when a wild animal devoured any of the flock it was required of Jacob, even when the loss occurred at night when it couldn't possibly be blamed on any negligence on the part of Jacob. It's clear that Laban preferred a poor and needy Jacob. A rich Jacob was of no use to him.

Does that sound cruel?

It's not unlike what many employers do today. Many people who work in banks will tell you as much. Every small shortage incurred out of inevitable human error is required of the tellers, many of whom walk away with less than half of their monthly pay as a result. But the same tellers also frequently report overages; but the banks will gleefully claim those.

Take the profits and pass on the losses is the capitalist's mantra.

Just so you know, when I talk of capitalists I do not mean it as an alternative to communists. That's not the context in which I employ the word. Just thought you should know that.

f) Trusts in his riches

Here is the man who did not make God his strength, but trusted in the abundance of his riches, and strengthened himself in his wickedness. (Psalms 52:7)

But Jesus answered again and said to them, "Children, how hard it is for those who trust in riches to enter the kingdom of God! (Mark 10:24)

Trust is a strong word. It's much deeper than just believing in the validity, genuineness or reality of something or someone. It's foundational. It's about where your confidence lies. It's about whom or what you fall back to when everything around you is shaken.

A foundation is the basis for everything. When the Twin Towers in New York came down tumbling their foundation stood. If there was a major tremor in your life and everything around you was moved, what would you be left with? That's what or who you trust.

King David says in Psalms 20 that *"some trust in chariots and some in horses, but we will remember the name of the Lord our God."*

In the book of Isaiah, God issues a warning to those who trust in man and military might.

"Woe to those who go down to Egypt for help, And rely on horses, Who

trust in chariots because they are many, And in horsemen because they are very strong, But who do not look to the Holy One of Israel, Nor seek the LORD! (Isaiah 31:1-3)

If you go to the jungles of Congo you will find teenage boys who have been raised amidst violence and have learnt to trust in the gun. All they need is a loaded weapon and they will get everything they want; from food to women. They guard their weapons with their lives. They know that if someone takes away their weapon, he has taken them out of the privileged class of oppressors and condemned them to the realm of the oppressed whose duty is to provide for the few who have guns. In such a setting, a gun — more like wealth in an organized capitalistic society —- is the symbol of status and authority; the very foundation of existence. And so they trust in it.

Likewise, as the Bible says, the rich man trusts in his wealth. He believes that he can get everything he wants through and because of it.

While most of the aforementioned characteristics of the rich man can exist in a poor person too, lurking beneath the surface and waiting to be unveiled when the first signs of wealth show up, it's only rich people who can trust in riches. The greater the riches, the bigger the temptation to trust in them.

*Do not **trust** in oppression, nor vainly **hope** in robbery; If riches increase, do not set your heart on them.* (Psalms 62:10)

Even if I am more concerned with the second part of the above verse, the first one is important for this context because it brings out three key words that describe the sort of trust that I am talking about. Look at the highlighted part of that scripture. Someone who trusts in wealth also has his hope in it and sets his heart on it. Those sound like progressive stages of trust. Notice that the latter stage which involves 'setting your heart' comes about when riches increase.

The temptation to trust in riches is just as real for Christians as it is for non-believers. That's why Paul wrote to Timothy with firm instructions for rich believers.

Command those who are rich in this present age not to be haughty, nor to trust in uncertain riches but in the living God, who gives us richly all things to enjoy. (1 Timothy 6:17)

It's obvious that he is talking about believers (what authority would Timothy have to command unbelievers?). But this verse doesn't just stop at warning rich folks, it also points out that God gives His children riches to enjoy. Isn't that wonderful?

It's possible to be rich and enjoy your wealth but still not trust in it, but in God.

When David says in the Psalms that he doesn't trust in horses and chariots it doesn't mean that he wins battles without them. He uses them alright. But he trusts in God, not in them.

The trust check

It's so easy for someone who started out trusting in God to wind up leaning on their riches, their power or their position when they acquire those things. It doesn't happen overnight. The slide is so gradual that the person involved will not notice that the foundation is shifting.

The rich man virus is stealth in its operation and all Christians must constantly check themselves for any tell tale signs.

There is nothing as uplifting as a good rags-to-riches story, especially when the journey has been about faith in God, who *"lifts the needy from the ash heap to make them sit with nobles, and inherit a seat of honor."* (I Samuel 2:8)

Unfortunately, such stories do not always have happy endings. Saul was lifted out from the smallest tribe and made king but wound up trusting in everything and everyone else but God. And so did Baasha.

Then the word of the LORD came to Jehu the son of Hanani, against Baasha, saying: "Inasmuch as I lifted you out of the dust and made you ruler over My people Israel, and you have walked in the way of Jeroboam, and have made My people Israel sin, to provoke Me to anger with their sins... (1 Kings 16: 1-2)

In much the same way, there are some men of God who started out with absolutely nothing but a word from God. But when they built great ministries and acquired honor and acceptance among society, they slowly drifted and now seem to depend more on their wealth, status or talent than on God. I do not say that with a critical spirit, or with anybody in mind. I am simply pointing out that the temptation to trust in wealth is so real even for well-meaning believers.

Thus says the LORD: "Let not the wise man glory in his wisdom, Let not the mighty man glory in his might, Nor let the rich man glory in his riches; (Jeremiah 9:23)

As God prospers His children, they must always check their foundation and make sure that it hasn't shifted. One easy way of knowing whom you trust is by considering whom you acknowledge for every small break. I will show you how trust and acknowledgment go together; first from the scriptures.

*Trust in the LORD with all your heart, And lean not on your own understanding; In all your ways **acknowledge** Him, And He shall direct your paths.* (Proverbs 3:5-6)

People who trust in God will acknowledge him for all their success. When you say a short prayer before you eat you acknowledge God as the provider.

Unbelievers never credit God for any of the good things that happen in their lives (it's always about them; their talent, wisdom or some unique insight they possess). But they will still blame Him for every natural disaster or family tragedy. Isn't it ironic how many so-called atheists will not waste an opportunity to pour scorn on a God they claim doesn't exist every time there is a massive calamity?

So who do you credit for your big breaks in life?

The Brazilian footballer Kaka famously wore a vest with the words: 'I belong to Jesus' under his jersey. In moments of euphoria, he lifted his shirt to expose those words to the cameras. It's his way of acknowledging God.

Of course his was a career that almost never was. He signed his first contract with Brazilian club Sao Paolo at the age of 15 but when he was 18 he suffered a catastrophic injury in his spine in a freak swimming pool accident and could have wound up paralyzed. But he was miraculously healed and ended up on the field pursuing his childhood dream of being a professional footballer. He's left the world in no doubt as to Whom he owes his career.

When he was unveiled as the world's best footballer in 2007, Kaka said that as a little boy he had only two dreams; he wanted to play professionally for Sao Paolo and play at least once for the Brazilian national team. But, he continued, the Bible says that God is able to give exceeding, abundantly above what you ask for. He played for much bigger clubs than his hometown outfit and featured so many times for his nation.

Who do you acknowledge in moments of elation? That should tell you something about who you trust.

g) Wise in his own eyes

The rich man is wise in his own eyes, But the poor who has understanding searches him out. (Proverbs 28:11)

The rich man creates a world around himself in which the only thing that matters is money. And since much of the world is chasing after money anyway, somebody who has none has little to offer.

In the years that I spent frolicking with extremely wealthy people, I noticed that they consider themselves to be experts on just about every subject under the sky, especially in comparison to someone like me who had no estates to show off. Without ever verbalizing it, it's clear that they think: "If you have so much knowledge why hasn't it made you rich?"

But the Bible says that a poor man who has understanding searches them out and in my case finds them shallow and superficial.

"Do not eat the bread of a miser," the Bible says. "Nor desire his delicacies. For as he thinks in his heart, so is he. 'Eat and drink,' he says to you, but his heart is not with you. The morsel you have eaten you will vomit up, *and waste your pleasant words.*" (Proverbs 23:6-8)

When a rich man asks a deep question the best answer you can offer is one feigning ignorance. Don't be tempted to think that he is interested in your insight. All he's doing is laying up a foundation for his next monologue. So just say enough to encourage him to keep on talking.

The book of Ecclesiastes speaks of a small city which was besieged by a great king. "Now there was found in it a poor wise man, and he by his wisdom delivered the city." Yet no one remembered him.

Then I said: "Wisdom is better than strength. Nevertheless the poor man's wisdom is despised, And his words are not heard. (Ecclesiastes 9:16)

h) Speaks like he owns tomorrow

Then He spoke a parable to them, saying: "The ground of a certain rich man yielded plentifully. And he thought within himself, saying, 'What shall I do, since I have no room to store my crops?' So he said, 'I will do this: I will pull down my barns and build greater, and there I will store all my crops and my goods. And I will say to my soul, "Soul, you have many goods laid up for many years; take your ease; eat, drink, and be merry."' But God said to him, 'Fool! This night your soul will be required of you; then whose will those things be which you have provided?'

"So is he who lays up treasure for himself, and is not rich toward God." (Luke 12: 16-21)

In a world governed by cupidity; one in which wealth is venerated far above everything else and is used interchangeably with success, those who possess it assume positions of infallibility. They are esteemed as beacons of wisdom and their opinions on diverse subjects are consumed as facts. With society elevating them to such heights, rich men often speak like they have attained a measure of immortality and they expect tomorrow to be theirs as a matter of right.

There's a reason why the scriptures often remind the rich man of his mortality and his inability to rescue himself through the vastness of his wealth.

Consider this wonderful portion of scripture from Psalms 49: 6-12 (Amp)

"Even of those who trust in and lean on their wealth and boast of the abundance of their riches?

None of them can by any means redeem [either himself or] his brother, nor give to God a ransom for him— For the ransom of a life is too costly, and [the price one can pay] can never suffice— So that he should live on forever and never see the pit (the grave) and corruption."

If the idea that money can purchase a person's soul seems foolish beyond comprehension to you — and I hope it does — that's because you are either unafflicted by the rich man virus or at worst are in the mild stages of the malaise.

But when wealth — the pursuit and enjoyment of it — gets to a person's head and, worse, his heart, it becomes his security. The frightful thing is that people who get into this pit don't even know when the downslide started.

In this degenerative state, wealth is no longer a means but an end; a path to immortality. The Psalmist goes ahead to describe the state of mind of such men.

"Their inward thought is that their houses will continue forever, and their dwelling places to all generations; they call their lands their own [apart from God] and after their own names."

Probably the biggest reason such people call their properties after their own name is because they are looking for immortality. The idea of extreme wealth birthing delusions of immortality is not entirely new to humanity. The tribe of Ephraim became very rich they declared that they had no sin.

Ephraim has said, Ah, but I have become rich; I have gained for myself wealth. All my profits shall bring on me no iniquity that would be sin. (But all his profits will never offset nor suffice to expiate the guilt which he has incurred.) (Hosea 12:8, Amp)

People who are intoxicated with wealth grow to believe that their earthly status should earn them some marks in the afterlife. Surely it must count for something! What sort of God would get rich, benevolent men who employed thousands of people and supported charitable causes and bunch them together with 'losers' in hell?

They are too important for that!

Now through science, the rich man is plotting for immortality through the so-called 2045 initiative. Depending on which side you stand, it's either the most audaciously insane load of baloney or the biggest work of scientific invention yet.

It's headed by a Russian media mogul named Dmitry Itskov who in July 2012 formally announced his intention to disembody men's conscious minds and upload them to a hologram—or an avatar— by 2045. He outlined a plan to achieve immortality by removing the human mind from the physical constraints presented by its biological human body and place it into a robot that can live forever.

What Itskov is calling cybernetic immortality and is planning to achieve through science was presented to the unsuspecting world through two blockbuster movies both released in 2009. Avatar, directed by James Cameroon, went ahead to break all box office records and became the highest-grossing film of all time. Surrogates, another science fiction epic directed by Jonathan Mostow, also portrayed a world in which people moved into surrogate bodies that neutralized the effects of age and pain.

What was presented as fictionalized art some years ago is now being sold to the world's wealthiest businessmen as a possibility within the realms of science. In his address to members of the Forbes billionaire's list on July 7, 2012, Itskov officially presented the 2045 Initiative promising them life without end, literally.

"You have worked hard... often even compromising your health and your longevity," he said. "And unfortunately, modern medicine is still the medicine of a hundred percent mortality – the best it can do is to temporarily delay the process of human ageing. But it no longer has to be this way."

Itskov went on to promise that his initiative "has the potential to free you, as well as the majority of all people on our planet, from disease, old age and even death."

In his appeal to the billionaires to support his project, the Russian said: "You also have the ability to finance the extension of your own life up to immortality. Our civilization has come very close to the creation of such technologies: it's not a science fiction fantasy. It is in your power to make sure that this goal will be achieved in your lifetime."

As far as this theory goes, when the rich people have worn out their physical bodies, their brains will be put in an 'avatar' or a robot. The new robotic being will have all the consciousness and memory of the previous person and can live forever unencumbered by the limitations of the natural body.

"One thing is clear," the 2045 Initiative website states "humanity, for the first time in its history, will make a fully managed evolutionary transition and eventually become a new species."

The world's obsession with evolution and the deification of Charles Darwin, as well as the often open hostility towards Bible truth is not just about explaining the past. It's more about trying to manage the future.

Now that science has managed to convince the secular world that we evolved from monkeys, it's time for the 'monkeys' to evolve to into avatars. May be then real monkeys will sit in a conference of their own in the beautiful forests of Uganda and discuss how they can also upgrade to humans, seeing as humans will have stepped up into immortal robots.

How could anybody believe something so ridiculous?

"*...Because although they knew God, they did not glorify Him as God, nor were thankful, but became futile in their thoughts, and their foolish hearts were darkened. **Professing to be wise, they became fools.** (Romans 1:21,22)*

Chapter 3

The deceitfulness of riches

*Now these are the ones sown among thorns; they are the ones who hear the word, and the cares of this world, the **deceitfulness of riches,** and the desires for other things entering in choke the word, and it becomes unfruitful.* (Mark 4:18-19)

Practically speaking, while it is yet in the ground, a seed cannot be pierced through with thorns. That can only happen when it has sprouted and grown into a plant. Therefore, within the context of this parable, the deceptive power of wealth is a danger to believers in whom the word (seed) has produced some effect. And the end thereof, as Jesus explained, is unfruitfulness.

My sister Winnie, when she was an upstart medical officer at a hospital in Kampala, witnessed firsthand how something seemingly innocuous can progress into an obsession. Every morning she was part of a group of doctors who walked into the ward to attend to patients. As a matter of principle, they gave priority to those in more urgent need. As a way of appreciation for the doctor's service, some patients offered a tip; nothing untoward, just simple gratitude expressed in monetary terms. They didn't have to give those tips because it is a government hospital and the doctors are paid by the line ministry.

But Winnie, who was born again and later became a pastor, told me that she felt the Holy Spirit leading her not to accept those tips. She couldn't understand why and neither could her colleagues who saw nothing wrong with it.

After a while, it became normal practice for some doctors to rush into the ward ahead of the rest and peruse through the patients looking for the apparently wealthier ones, whom they would attend to in anticipation of a decent tip. They could tell rich patients from poor ones by the adornments around their bed and the number of their attendants.

Over time, the more affluent patients got priority even if their conditions were not urgent.

And so doctors who started out by simply accepting tips grew to anticipate them and then upgraded to expecting them, until finally they started demanding for them. They would lavish their care on tipping patients and reserve a cold, caustic attitude for those who couldn't or wouldn't tip.

A year later, all the noticeably poor patients were left to Winnie's care while her colleagues shared out the posh ones. She was the only one for whom the class disparity didn't make a difference because she wasn't going to accept the tip anyway. Then she understood why she had been led that way, and so did the other believing doctors who had previously thought of her as unnecessarily straitlaced. They found themselves too entrapped in the tipping culture and too dependent on its rewards to free themselves.

Never underestimate the power of progression. The rich man virus has used it to devastating effect and overthrown the faith of many.

Many believers have to stand guard every day over the allure of mammon. Their faith and their resolve to stay true to their principles is regularly tested to its limit. Some work for financial institutions, at revenue collection depots or for clearing and forwarding agencies. They watch many of their colleagues and even subordinates amass wealth through under-declaration, non-disclosure and other devious means. Through continued practice, these fraudulent procedures often become the norm and, over time, the line between right and wrong is so blurred that only the most cutting-edge believers will still notice it.

While they live off modest salaries, barely clearing the bills, everyone around them is building a lavish country home, schooling their children at the costliest institutions and mapping out luxurious vacation destinations. Their colleagues often torment and ridicule them, dismissing them as prissy.

"All you have to do," they are constantly reminded, "is to relax your morals just a little".

There is nothing particularly new or unique about a scenario in which the wicked appear to prosper and use their abundance to torment the righteous man who will not indulge.

In fact, the Psalmist describes it in the 73rd Psalm.

"But as for me, my feet had almost stumbled; my steps nearly slipped. For I was envious of the boastful, when I saw the prosperity of the wicked

"They are not in trouble as other men, nor are they plagued like other men. Therefore pride serves as their necklace....Their eyes bulge with abundance; they have more than heart could wish. They scoff and speak wickedly concerning oppression; they speak loftily. They set their mouth against the heavens, and their tongue walks through the earth." (v2-9)

Love one, despise the other

Money is a good servant but a cruel master.

But money is never content to stay a servant. It wants to be the master.

It is always plotting for the throne of a man's heart. That's where it thinks it belongs. If left unchecked, it can easily turn the tables on a believer who once possessed it until it possesses him. It employs stealth methods to achieve its aim.

Jesus said: *"No one can serve two masters... for he will hate the one and love the other, or else he will be loyal to one and despise the other. You cannot serve God and mammon."* (Matthew 6:24)

Most Bible translations refer to mammon as money, wealth or possessions, which for the most part is accurate. But in Greek tradition, an important consideration at the time the New Testament was written, Mammon was the name of the god that governed wealth, greed and avarice. He was personified as an object of worship. So mammon is not just wealth or the allure of it, he is a spiritual personality with a peculiar identity that always demands to be a master.

Like God, mammon demands complete loyalty and worship. That's why Jesus makes it an either-or proposition. You either serve Him or mammon. No in-betweens.

The deceitfulness of riches

Mammon is a unique thing; and I will explain why.

There are so many habits, many of them of a sinful nature, that are designed to distract a Christian from complete surrender to the Holy Spirit. When these habits become a driving force in our lives and start competing for attention with God they qualify to be called idols. It may be sport, television, politics, career or whatever it is that seems to draw your attention more than the pursuit of deep fellowship with God. Even the noblest things like Christian ministry and charity can become idols if not well managed.

Many Christians live with these idols but remain, for the most part, loyal to God. The story of Jacob in Genesis illustrates that. After living with his uncle Laban for two decades and being married to his two daughters who cherished their pagan fetishes, Jacob had grown to accommodate foreign gods in his household. But he still heard from and obeyed God.

Then God said to Jacob, "Arise, go up to Bethel and dwell there; and make an altar there to God, who appeared to you when you fled from the face of Esau your brother." (Genesis 35:1-4)

And Jacob said to his household and to all who were with him, "Put away the foreign gods that are among you, purify yourselves, and change your garments. Then let us arise and go up to Bethel; and I will make an altar there to God, who answered me in the day of my distress and has been with me in the way which I have gone." So they gave Jacob all the foreign gods which were in their hands, and the earrings which were in their ears; and Jacob hid them under the terebinth tree which was by Shechem.

Jacob worshipped the God of his grandfather Abraham, even if he had foreign gods in his house (I suppose that's why they are called foreign). But when he put them away, he entered into a deeper covenant with God, who at that point changed his name from Jacob to Israel.

For a Christian, some of these idols might be outright sinful; immoral or fraudulent behavior, foul speech, anger, bitterness, jealousy or the like. But they are still 'foreign gods' because you still serve the God of Abraham. I am not trying to trivialize any of those habits. Like Jacob, we all have to put those 'foreign gods' under the terebinth tree (read the cross) if we are to enter a deeper experience with God. But that is besides the point of this book.

The purpose of that background is to show you that to the best of my knowledge there is no habit, sinful or otherwise, no distraction or failure that the Bible places in the same category as Mammon. He is not just a distraction, he is a master. The god of money demands loyalty, total allegiance and worship. Jesus faced him during the temptation of the desert when the devil made Him three propositions recorded in scripture (Math 4:1-10).

I believe that there are three different classes of demons behind each temptation.

"If you are the son of God command these stones to become bread…"

The biggest word in that proposal is 'if' and it's aimed at making Jesus doubt His identity.

When He passed that one, the hierarchy of the tempter and

the temptation moved a notch higher. *"If you are the Son of God, throw yourself down. For it is written…."*

I believe that is a call to pride. Since Jesus knew who He was, the devil wanted Him to think like; "Well, I am Jesus, the Son of God, I can pretty much do what I please and the host of angels will be there for me."

When the Lord passed that one too, Satan called back his regular army and sent out his Republican Guard, so to speak; his master card: mammon.

"Again the devil took Him to an exceedingly high mountain, and showed Him all the kingdoms of the world and their glory. And he said to Him, "All these things I will give You if You will fall down and worship me."

Notice that the demon that offers wealth, power and glory demands worship. None of the other tempting devils asked Jesus to prostrate and worship them; but mammon demands to be the master. He doesn't just come to shake your faith with the 'if' word like the lower class of devils which first tempted Jesus. If mammon had the audacity to demand worship from Christ, then he will most definitely demand it from Christians.

It's no wonder then that Jesus calls mammon a master. *"No one can serve two masters…You cannot serve God and mammon.*

There is nothing quite like money that entices, cajoles, corrupts and then draws the hearts of men away from the love of God and gives them a completely new DNA.

I know you must be thinking 'how could I possibly bow down and worship a devil?'

But the proposal is never presented that bluntly. Mammon is a lot more stealth in his operations.

Despising God

Remember Jesus said; *He will be loyal to one and despise the other. You cannot serve God and mammon."*

Stop for a while and think about the weight of the word despise. It is one thing to deny, ignore, abuse or even hate God. I know many people who started that way but ended up serving Him. To despise God, however, is such a shocking state for anyone, much less a Christian to find themselves in. The thought of it gives me goose pimples.

I am sure you are thinking: 'nothing could possibly make me despise God.'

But that's never the starting point; it's the destination.

And the journey is protracted.

The danger with such gradual progression is that it thrives on inactivity; it requires little or no input from the backslider. No Christian is ever going to consciously do anything that will make him despise God. The devil knows as much so he never presents it that way. It's delivered in small seemingly harmless baits. Only the first step is significant. The rest are seamless. Satan is the master of such craft. He designs his deceit in such a way that all it takes for it to thrive is for the targeted victim to do nothing.

I read the story of a man who met a Servant of God long ago and agreed to become his protégé. They served together for over three years and the Master trusted him with his money bag because they had become friends. But after a while, the disciple started despising the Master. I am sure you have read about that man too. His name is Judas.

I am convinced that Judas Iscariot didn't start out as a betrayer. His intentions were probably as noble as all the other disciples at the start. When Jesus sent them out in pairs, Judas was also preaching the gospel of the kingdom, casting out devils and healing the sick with as much fervor. When they returned bubbling with excitement to relate to Jesus how the devils fled at the mention of His name, Judas Iscariot was probably just as enchanted as them all.

So at what point did it he cross the line?

He didn't! Not at any one point. It is a process.

Judas had a weakness and he indulged it. The other disciples had weaknesses too and for the most part they indulged theirs too. But unlike the rest, Judas' weakness was for money. Mammon, as I have already shown you, is a master. He goes for complete, not partial conquests.

The journey from disciple to betrayer starts with a seemingly innocuous invitation to pick a few nickels from the money box. Judas probably had a good explanation to back up his action; something like a family emergency. Or maybe he convinced himself that he was only borrowing and would pay it back soon. Besides, nobody was going to notice because Jesus' money box was never in short supply. They always had enough to give to the poor. The Bible says as much.

….Then Jesus said to him, "What you do, do quickly." But no one at the table knew for what reason He said this to him. For some thought, because Judas had the money box, that Jesus had said to him, "Buy those things we need for the feast," or that he should give something to the poor. (John 13:26-29)

The only reason they would suppose that Jesus was sending Judas to give to the poor is because it was something He frequently did.

So for a while Judas was simply pilfering the collections. Nothing 'too serious'.

Have you ever noticed that most of the other prominent disciples had imperfections too? But they were largely concealed until the moment Jesus dropped the bombshell that He was going to die. It was a really trying moment for all of them.

They had abandoned their jobs when Jesus came calling. For some, like Matthew the tax collector, those jobs had been lucrative. For the most part they had enjoyed the journey. They had believed that Jesus was the Messiah and had enjoyed seeing Him heal the sick, raise the dead and confound the Pharisees with His wisdom.

Like most Jews at the time, and up to now, the disciples interpreted the concept of the Messiah sitting on the throne of David as political authority. They expected Him to be king in the earthly sense. That was the prevailing belief and it was behind Herod's pursuit of the young Jesus, as well as the reaction of the multitudes towards His miracles.

Consider this for a typical crowd reaction.

"Then those men, when they had seen the sign that Jesus did, said, "This is truly the Prophet who is to come into the world. Therefore when Jesus perceived that they were about to come and take him by force to make Him king, he departed again to a mountain by Himself alone." (John 6:14-15)

As soon as the five thousand people who had been filled

with five loaves and two fish entertained the idea that He was the Christ, they wanted to forcefully hand Him the throne which in their minds was His destiny.

Even the disciples expected Him to become an earthly King. They said as much on the road to Emmaus, when two of them unknowingly spoke to the risen Christ. *"But we were hoping that it was He who was going to redeem Israel."* (Luke 24:21).

Right up to the time of his ascension to heaven, the disciples were convinced that he was going to wield some political power. "Therefore when they had come together, they asked Him saying, *"Lord, will you at this time restore the kingdom to Israel?"* (Acts 1:6)

So for all the while they walked with Jesus, they probably imagined that the miracles were but a preamble to the real thing; a sort of campaign strategy to get Him the throne of David. They were probably going to become governors to rule with Him. They would be the envy of everyone. But their delusions of grandeur were shattered when Jesus broke the news of His impending death. Then all their weakness came out fresh like they always do in moments of uncertainty.

Peter, the spontaneous talker who seemed to speak first and think later, took Him aside and began to rebuke Him, saying "Far be it from You, Lord; this shall not happen to You!"

As far as Peter was concerned, Jesus was probably developing cold feet and letting up on His destiny. And tied within Jesus' destiny were Peter's own ambitions. Of course the Bible doesn't spell it out in those words, but Jesus' response to Peter tells you something about where the disciples were coming from.

*But He turned and said to Peter, "Get behind Me, Satan! You are an offense to Me, for you are **not mindful of the things of God, but the things of men**.*" (Matt 16:23)

James and John, the two sons of Zebedee, pulled Him aside and made a special request that they may sit on the right and left of Jesus in His glory. It's not clear if they meant Jesus' glory in heaven or the one they expected him to inherit as the Redeemer of Israel sitting on the earthly throne of David. Whatever they meant, the other disciples were displeased because there was a simmering power struggle which Jesus had to address.

John showed that he was zealous to keep intruders out of their close enclave when he said: *"Teacher, we saw someone who does not follow us casting out demons in Your name, and we forbade him because he does not follow us."* (Mark 9:38)

I imagine the last thing John wanted were backdoor entrants into their group.

As Jesus continued talking about his impending departure, Simon Peter was compelled to ask: "Lord, where are You going?"

Imagine what was going through his mind. 'Where does all this leave us? Are we supposed to write off three years of our lives and go back to the seashore? Shall we even find our boats after all this time away?'

So when Jesus said that Peter could only follow Him later, he replied:

"Lord, why can I not follow you now?"

Jesus continued: *"And where I go you know, and the way you know."*

The other disciples were also left in a spin. Thomas, who

was later shown as a doubter, first divulged his skeptical nature at this point when he asked: "Lord, we do not know where you are going, and how can we know the way?"

When Jesus told them that He is going to the Father, Phillip said: *"Lord, show us the Father, and it is sufficient for us."*

I am trying to show you that in this moment of uncertainty, the disciples' insecurities were exposed in their rawest form. Nonetheless, all but one of them recovered to play their part in the establishment of the New Testament church. Even as they fled in the night, denied Jesus, doubted, went back to their old life, right back to the seashore where Jesus first found them (John 21:3), the disciples remained loyal in their hearts to Jesus.

The only one who fell away permanently and lost his place was the one whose weakness was for money. Mammon doesn't settle for partial conquests. He goes for the kill.

Now I will use the story of Judas to show you how mammon works.

Then Mary took a pound of very costly oil of spikenard, anointed the feet of Jesus, and wiped His feet with her hair. And the house was filled with the fragrance of the oil. But one of His disciples, Judas Iscariot, Simon's son, who would betray Him, said, "Why was this fragrant oil not sold for three hundred denarii and given to the poor?" This he said, not that he cared for the poor, but because he was a thief, and had the money box; and he used to take what was put in it. (John 12:3-6)

In the accounts of Matthew (26:8) and Mark (14:4), it is said that he was moved with indignation and said: *"Why waste this oil?"*

That statement is loaded with sneering overtones. Judas

quickly estimated the value of the perfume and found it to be worth three hundred denarii (about a year's wages for labor).

Mary, the sister of Lazarus who had just been raised from the dead, probably knew that Jesus was about to be killed. The Bible says she had kept the oil to use it for the time of His embalming (John 12: 7 Amp). It was this same Mary who had sat at Jesus' feet to listen to His words while her sister Martha served food. Knowing that the Lord was going to die (He was crucified within a fortnight of that day), Mary picked out her prized perfume and anointed His feet. But the significance of the moment was lost on Judas Iscariot who couldn't see beyond the value of the oil. A perfume that sets you back a year's wages is expensive alright. But no matter the cost, perfumes are made to be used on people. There is no more appropriate use for perfumes, is there? So why does Judas think that it is wasted on Jesus?

If I baked a nice cake and gave it to a pig you could say 'what a waste'. But if I gave the cake to a person and you made the same statement you would be implying that he/she is undeserving of something so good. That would be someone you think lowly of, or despise.

So when Judas cries out 'what a waste!' he is in effect saying that such a costly ointment should be used on someone more deserving. Of course he uses the classic excuse of the poor, suggesting that the perfume be sold and the money given to the poor, but he didn't care for the poor. The Bible says as much. In any case, it was his responsibility to give to the poor and the money would be in his care. What Judas was saying is 'why waste something so valuable on someone so undeserving'.

The deceitfulness of riches

Clearly he had grown to despise Jesus. That's what mammon can do. Remember what Jesus said about serving two masters; be loyal to one and despise the other.

It all started with simple pilfering from the money bag but look where it ended.

At that stage of his backsliding, Judas' heart was darkened enough to accomplish the devil's grand plan. It took him years to go from disciple to despiser and eventually to betrayer of Jesus.

While James and John were jostling for positions at either side of Jesus, Peter was preparing to go back fishing and Phillip was asking for the way, Judas was imagining how much money he could make off Jesus' death.

Judas probably justified his action by thinking: "He is going to die anyway. He said so Himself. So I might as well make the most of it. I didn't initiate the plot to kill Him, neither am I going to execute it. I am just the innocent guy pointing the killers to their target. That's all. And while I am it, I could get myself some prime property."

I have always wondered what was going through Judas' mind when he arrived with the soldiers and kissed Jesus. I guess at that point every sense of guilt had gone. The biggest act of treachery had, in his darkened heart, been immaculately dressed up as a shrewd business deal.

If the devil had made the proposal for Judas to betray Jesus much earlier, when Judas was casting out demons in Jesus' name, he too would be cast out with the other demons. But mammon is craftier than that. He starts with a misdemeanor, which burgeons into a habit, then a craving all the way downhill and the victim never notices at what stage he or she started despising God.

Chapter 4

Easier for a camel

*N*ow *a certain ruler asked Him, saying, "Good Teacher, what shall I do to inherit eternal life?"*

So Jesus said to him, "Why do you call Me good? No one is good but One, that is, God. You know the commandments: 'Do not commit adultery,' 'Do not murder,' 'Do not steal,' 'Do not bear false witness,' 'Honor your father and your mother.' "

*And he said, "**All these things I have kept from my youth**."*

*So when Jesus heard these things, He said to him, "You are still lack one thing. **Sell all that you have and distribute to the poor, and you will have treasure in heaven; and come, follow Me**." (Luke 18: 18-26)*

*But when he heard this, **he became very sorrowful, for he was very rich**.*

*And when Jesus saw that he became very sorrowful, He said, "How hard it is for those who have riches to enter the kingdom of God! For it is easier for a camel to go through the eye of a needle than for **a rich man** to enter the kingdom of God."*

And those who heard it said, "Who then can be saved?"

No single statement by Jesus has caused more confusion over the centuries on the subject of wealth in Christendom than: *"it is easier for a camel to go through the eye of a needle than for a rich man to enter the Kingdom of God."* And it is recorded in three gospel accounts.

It's no wonder the disciples who heard it were "astonished" and wondered; "who then can be saved?"

The disciples were confused because the Jewish culture of the time prized material wealth and viewed it as God's reward for obedience. And with good reason too.

From Abraham through the Law, the Prophets, down to the New Covenant, God promises a blessing. And Proverbs 10:22 says that: *"The blessing of the Lord makes one rich."*

It didn't take long for God's blessing on Abram promised in Genesis 12 to yield wealth. In fact, it took only one chapter because it says in Genesis 13:2 that *"Abram was very rich in livestock, in silver and in gold."*

The Law promises a great blessing and wealth for the obedience (Deuteronomy 15) as do the prophets. Isaiah 1:19 states that: *"If you are willing and obedient, you shall eat the good of the land."*

The New Covenant promises the blessing of Abraham to those in Christ (Gal 3:14), while 2Cor 8:9 says: "For you know the grace of our Lord Jesus Christ, that though He was rich, yet for your sakes He became poor, that you through His poverty might become rich."

But then, why does God want His people to be rich when "it is easier for a camel to go through the eye of a needle than for a rich man to enter the kingdom of God?"

Why did Jesus seem to attach such an apparent deterrent to riches?

What a paradox!

There have been diverse historical and intellectual attempts to explain what Jesus meant but all these centuries later believers are just as astonished as the disciples were back then.

A common teaching I have heard many times alludes to a narrow gate in the old Jerusalem called the 'eye of a needle'. As far as this theory goes, a camel could not pass through that gate unless it stooped low and first had all its baggage removed. After dark, when the main gates of the city were closed, travelers used this smaller gate through which the camel could only enter crawling on its knees. That story has been the premise of many tear-jerking sermons about coming to God on our knees, unencumbered by any weight. It's an interesting theory no doubt but, sadly, a false one too.

Firstly, there are some historical accounts that dispute the existence of such a gate. But that is hardly the basis of my argument. If Jesus was referring to a small gate into the city, the disciples, who were no strangers to Jerusalem, would have known about it. They would also have known that late-arriving camels frequently went through it, albeit with some difficulty.

But that is hardly a reason for anyone to be greatly astonished to the point of asking Him "who then can be saved?"

While the Jews esteemed wealth, the Greek culture of the time treated it with suspicion at best but was mostly indifferent or outright disdainful of it. Greek philosopher Plato was known to be emphatic in his distaste for money. And even if other famous philosophers, particularly Aristotle, had a more complimentary view of wealth, the Platonic view of the soul being above the body and money being beneath both is an attitude that was passed into the Christian moral tradition and has always figured among moral assumptions of religious folk.

The vow of poverty embraced by the Roman Catholic Church since the 12th Century is derived from the same parable of the rich young man who came to Jesus asking what he must do to inherit eternal life. In the account of Matthew, Jesus said: *"If you want to be perfect go, sell what you have and give to the poor…and come and follow me."* (Matt 19:21).

And so the Catholic Church came up with 'three evangelical counsels' to be undertaken by people who want to live a perfect or consecrated life. Poverty is one of them. Chastity and obedience are the others.

It is an attitude that similarly guided the socialist views of the 19th Century Western novelists who were relatively poor but dismissed rich merchants as people who had chosen a low life because they couldn't match up to the nobler values of intellectualism.

All that confusion concerning the rich young ruler's story evaporates when you understand what the Bible means by 'a rich man'. It doesn't mean anybody who happens to be rich.

Consider another story that, in the gospel account of Luke, comes immediately after the rich young ruler who was told to sell all his goods.

Even if the events recorded in Luke didn't necessary happen in the time order in which they are presented, I believe the Holy Spirit had these stories following each other for a reason.

Then Jesus entered and passed through Jericho. Now behold, there was a man named **Zacchaeus who was a chief tax collector, and he was rich**. *And he sought to see who Jesus was, but could not because of the crowd, for he was of short stature. So he ran ahead and climbed up into a sycamore tree to see Him, for He was going to pass that way. And when Jesus came to the place, He looked up and saw him, and said to him, "Zacchaeus, make haste and come down, for today I must stay at your house." So he made haste and came down, and received Him joyfully.* **But when they saw it, they all complained, saying, "He has gone to be a guest with a man who is a sinner."**

Then Zacchaeus stood and said to the Lord, "Look, Lord, I give **half of my goods to the poor***; and if I have taken anything from anyone by false accusation, I restore fourfold."* (Luke 19:1-8:)

Now consider the similarities and, especially, the differences between the protagonists of the two parables and the intriguing way in which Jesus handled both.

1. **DESCRIPTION**: The story of the rich young ruler appears in all but one gospel but his name is not mentioned. None of the people who are afflicted with the rich man virus is mentioned by name in any of the parables or narrations that speak of them. Not one.

The rich man in the story of Lazarus is only known as such. And so are all the other rich men in all the gospel accounts. That is a clear allusion to their loss of identity. I have already shown you that one of the characteristics of the rich man is that his wealth becomes his identity. It's no wonder then that the Bible simply refers to people afflicted with the rich man virus as "a rich man".

By contrast, the Bible tells us a lot more about Zacchaeus (mentioned by name). We know about his stature and we know that he was a chief tax collector. Notice that the Bible doesn't use the phrase 'a rich man'. It says "… and he was rich". Which means there was a lot more to him that his wealth.

2. **BACKGROUND**: The rich young ruler was an adherent and in all likelihood a role model. He had grown up in the knowledge of God and obeyed all commandments. He had acquired his vast wealth the right way, defrauding no one (the commandments he professed to have obeyed from his youth cover theft and all).

    Zacchaeus, on the other hand, was a rebel. He had acquired his wealth through larceny and was probably the personification of tax-collector greed and hedonism.

3. **PUBLIC REACTION**: When Jesus mentioned, in clear reference to the rich young ruler, that it is easier for a camel to go through the eye of a needle than for a rich man to enter the kingdom of God, the crowd was

in shock. "Who then can be saved?" they gasped. They knew him as a very good, devout man, the kind who would pass any human test for entry into the kingdom. He was humble too. The gospel of Mark says he knelt down before Jesus. So if such a man is disqualified, then who can qualify for the kingdom of God?

The reaction of the crowd when Jesus announced that he was going to dine at Zacchaeus' house couldn't have been in starker contrast. They complained. What business could Jesus possibly have with such a notorious thief?

4. **JESUS' VERDICT**: Now here's where the shock is. Jesus tells the rich ruler that he must sell ALL that he has, distribute the money to the poor and follow Him. That is not a cut-across prerequisite for salvation. But it was a prerequisite for this particular man.

By contrast, Jesus never asked Zacchaeus to surrender any of his wealth, but the tax collector volunteered to give only half of it and yet got his salvation.

Humanly speaking, if anybody had to give up his entire estate it should have been Zacchaeus, who had acquired it fraudulently. But he wasn't required to, and he didn't. Yet he got salvation that day and was a joyous man. Instead, a man who got his money through legitimate means, obeying all known commandments while at it, was required to give it all up. He didn't and didn't get salvation, at least not that time. He left filled with sorrow and Jesus' accompanying words were: "It's easier for a camel to go through the eye of a needle...."

Why the disparity?

It comes down to what place wealth has in a man's heart — or if it has any place at all — because it shouldn't. The Psalmist says: "when riches increase do not set your heart on them."

Zacchaeus demonstrated that his money had no control over him. Without any prompting, he stood up and announced his generous plan of restitution. I have heard it said that God doesn't have a man's heart until he has his wallet. I believe that to be true. Money is usually the final frontier of man's resistance to God's authority. So when Zacchaeus had his moment of epiphany and decided to restore all he had stolen, and four times over, his final line of resistance had been broken.

And Jesus said to him, "Today salvation has come to this house, because he also is a son of Abraham..." Luke 19:9

The rich young ruler's case was different and so was his prescription. He had a deep attachment to his wealth. In spite of his piety and spotless outward demeanor, his heart was afflicted with the rich man virus. His wealth had become his stronghold; a part of him that he wasn't ready to surrender. He wasn't just rich; he was a rich man, and what a big difference that makes in the wider context of this book. Behind the slightly different alignment of words lies a seismic shift in attitude.

The rich ruler's heart was encased; and no caging is as robust and nearly impenetrable as mammon. Yet it had to be broken for Christ to have any entry into the young ruler's heart. For that to happen he had to surrender the object of his affection; his wealth.

He probably thought that Jesus was going to give another

commandment which he could add onto the cartload of those he had obeyed since his youth. But Jesus wanted to occupy the place in his heart that was reserved for his wealth. So the rich ruler left a sad man because he wasn't quite ready to dethrone mammon and enthrone Christ.

Chapter 5

Vaccination against the rich man virus

Elvis was lying on his couch watching a television program he likes on Crime and Investigation Channel when he saw a white horse towering above him. He heard a voice inviting him to mount the horse. He was caught in the spirit and rode the stallion on an expansive flat ground on an overcast night. A long distance away he could see a group of people carrying a heavy load on their heads. It weighed them down and made them trudge along slowly and arduously. He could tell that they were believers. Above them a thick cloud was gathering and a storm was looming.

As he got closer he made out to see what sort of load they

were bearing. He got close enough to see that the load had the label 'the love of money'.

He heard the same voice tell him to go and chop down the burden; and so he did. Then this group of believers was relieved and walked straight and with renewed freedom. Suddenly, the heavens which were thick over them opened up and it started to rain heavily. Only this wasn't ordinary rain; it was raining money.

Elvis Mbonye is a prophet friend of mine. The message from his vision is as clear as daylight. The only thing that is holding the children of God from experiencing unusual financial success is the love of money.

About mid 2010 I was studying on the subject of deliverance from the book of Exodus. My specific text of interest for this study was from the ten plagues in Egypt that cracked Pharaoh's stone heart. It's a fascinating tale of two men trying to show who has a more powerful God through demonstrations of power.

It starts with Pharaoh asking Moses: *"Who is Yahweh that I should obey His voice to let Israel go? I do not know Yahweh, nor will I let Israel go."* (Ex 5:2)

Then Pharaoh reacted by increasing the yoke on the Israelites. *"Why do you take the people from their work,"* he told Moses and Aaron. *"Get back to your labor."*

He proceeded to say of the Israelites that: *"they are idle; therefore they cry out, saying 'Let us go and sacrifice to our God. "Let more work be laid on the men, that they may labor in it, and let them not regard false words."*

Everything said in that portion of scripture represents the

devil's plan for Christians and their finances. He wants them to work so hard to barely meet their needs — if at all — so that they have no time to serve God and study His word. Sadly, many Christians are caught in that trap. Their desire to serve God is alive and active, but they are weighed down with labor, every spare moment spent trying to pay the next pending bill. The devil loves the sight of believers wasting their lives in the pursuit of a meager existence; their authority and inheritance in God all sacrificed for the next salary.

Eventually, some believers get into a lowly state of non-expectation in which the best they can hope for is a measure of comfort in slavery. That is precisely what happened with the Israelites.

"Then as they (the Hebrew leaders) came out from Pharaoh, they met Moses and Aaron who stood there to meet them. And they said to them, "Let the Lord look on you and judge, because you have made us abhorrent in the sight of Pharaoh and in the sight of his servants, to put a sword in their hand to kill us." (Ex 5:20-21)

Curiously, these were the same Hebrew leaders who, when they first heard that God had seen their affliction and visited Moses, bowed their heads and worshipped. But when Pharaoh tightened the screw and forced them to make the same quota of bricks without straw, they quickly reverted back to their shell, hoping for the best conditions in their servitude; all illusions of freedom quickly abandoned.

I know many such Christians and I am sure so do you; who read or listen to the word preached and entertain grand dreams of financial security. They have a plan to serve God in a way they believe they've been called to. Some stop at the plan, some even step out believing that financial security will come when they step into God's plan. But when the trials come — and they most definitely do — a majority of them go back to the security of servitude, tormented each day by the inner realization that they have sacrificed their calling for paid labor.

A few, however, press through the period of making the same quota of bricks without any straw provided, and they are the ones who enjoy the sweet pleasure of living an abundant life; earning more than they need while actually doing what they enjoy and what they are called to do.

Moses was undeterred by the antipathy of the Hebrew leaders and progressively demonstrated that the Egyptian gods were no match for Yahweh. Pharaoh slowly started caving in. But the Lord continued to harden his heart to show us the obstinacy of Satan.

After the first few plagues, Pharaoh allowed Israel to sacrifice to their God, but only in the land of Egypt. Moses refused to settle for that. More plagues ensued.

Then Pharaoh said, okay I will let you go in the wilderness, only do not go very far away. It's natural for the devil to want you to stay within reach, where he can continually torment you.

Then after a few more plagues Pharaoh was willing to let only the men go.

Every plague represents Yahweh's triumph over and humiliation of another Egyptian god; from the defiling of the River Nile which was an object of Egyptian worship, through frogs, which represented the god of fertility, to the sun, which was a symbol of Pharaoh's personal god.

So after enduring three days of pitch darkness, Pharaoh was reasonably subdued.

So he called to Moses and said: *"Go serve the Lord; only let your flocks and your herds be kept back."*

That was progress. From his original mulishness their tormentor had now opened the gates for them to leave, along with the wives and children. Many Christians would have cut a deal right there and fled before he changed his mind. Not Moses.

The servant of Yahweh replied: *"Our livestock shall also go with us; not a hoof shall be left behind."*

A dialogue which started with Pharaoh asking "who is Yahweh that I should obey him?" ends with Yahweh declaring that: *"Against all the gods of Egypt I will execute judgment (tomorrow.) I am the Lord."* (Ex 12:12)

With every other condition met by Pharaoh, it's important to note that the final plague, the death of the first born, was meant to rescue the wealth of Israel. That's how important His children's wealth is to God. As you all know, they didn't just rescue their flocks, they plundered the Egyptians too.

I took time to meditatively think about how terror-stricken the Egyptians were to have gone into their houses and unburied the chests of gold and silver and willfully handed them over to their erstwhile slaves, imploring them to leave their country.

As I meditated on it, the Holy Spirit told me: "You cannot plunder Egypt and stay in Egypt."

There's no way Israel could have taken the wealth of Egypt and enjoyed it right there in Egypt. Sadly, that's what so many

The Rich Man Virus

Christians are trying to do. They want God's prosperity alright, but they want to enjoy it in a worldly way; gratifying their most carnal desires.

Just look around and you will see believers whose attitude towards money is not far divorced from that of the world. They too think of wealth as a symbol of power and glory; an invitation to prodigal indulgence. They want to plunder Egypt and stay in Egypt.

The Israelites were like that too. They didn't mind picking the silver, gold and clothing off the Egyptians. They were quick to obey when Moses told them to raid the Egyptian homes with requests for wealth. But a few days into their desert journey they were talking about electing someone to lead them back to Egypt. In their naivety they imagined that they could go right back and enjoy their new-found status as free men and women, wearing the gold necklaces and laced clothes while living next door to the people who once owned those items.

The Bible says that God gives us richly all things to enjoy (1 Tim 6:17). But it's a person's definition of 'enjoy' that will determine who walks in God's abundant prosperity and who stops at talking about it. If the word 'enjoy' arouses in you all manner of sinful, hedonistic imaginations then I suggest you work on getting your soul out of Egypt because you cannot plunder Egypt and stay in Egypt. The wealth transfer will materialize for all those who are willing to leave Pharaoh's land.

Ntale's tale

He raises the poor out of the dust, And lifts the needy out of the ash heap, (Psalms 113:6-8)

That He may seat him with princes— With the princes of His people.

I haven't met anyone for whom that scripture rings truer than Francis Ntale. I doubt I ever will.

Ntale is an effervescent and easily likeable character whom I first met sometime in the mid months of 2011. He is a man who has plunged such unimaginable depths of poverty and suffered every kind of humiliation that results from deprivation. Yet he emerged from it unscathed, bubbling with ebullience and a wonderful sense of humor. Even if he intends them to be funny, and presents them as such, tales of his former destitution are so harrowing that even poor people are moved to tears.

Ntale's journey from the literal abyss started with tears of surrender one evening in 1997.

At the time he was working as a waiter at a food stall in the market in Masaka, a town in the central region of Uganda. Actually the word waiter is a bit of a misnomer in his case, because his daily brief involved getting orders from people who preferred to have lunch in their shops and then often crossing the road with a tray to deliver the food. People who do such work are called food transporters, a name which carries a whole load of derision in the local language. He had a wife and six children and they lived in one room in the most rundown suburb of the town.

One day Ntale heard that someone was selling a shamba

not too far away from town for 400,000 shillings. Even in a rural setting, that was a bargain. But it was way out of Ntale's natural reach. So he decided to believe God. Every so often he and his wife would walk around the piece of land and pray earnestly that it remains unsold until they were ready to buy it. For the land to have remained unsold and still on sale for two years was a miracle in itself.

One fine day, they pulled out their motley collection of coins and creased bank notes which had been accrued from the sale of every valuable household item and more than two years of rigorous saving and, finally, they had hit the magic figure. The following day the land of promise would finally be theirs. They praised God.

But in the midst of the praise which was understandably fervent that night, the Lord spoke to Ntale. The instructions were clear as the daylight. He paused and suddenly wore a forlorn look. His wife noticed and asked him what was wrong.

"Nothing," he replied.

He woke up unusually early the following morning and headed for town, from where he took a bus to Kyazanga, a trading centre about an hour's ride down the same highway. That's where he met a pastor called Luka.

Pastor Luka had a good job working for the Uganda Revenue Authority when God told him to quit and start a church in Kyazanga. He said God had promised to take care of him financially. The 400,000 shillings which the Lord had instructed Ntale to give him was the beginning of the fulfillment of that promise. But for Ntale it was a real dagger in the heart. He was in tears when he handed it over. They both were.

Vaccination against the rich man virus

It was an anxious ride back home for Ntale. What was he going to tell his wife? The land had been a life dream for her. She had fantasized over it, over the big house and extra land to cultivate and feed her family. How would she react?

What if he had heard wrong? Was it really the voice of God? Why would God keep the land from being sold for a whole two years then ask him to give the money? His mind was filled with so many uncertainties.

"Where's the purchase agreement," his wife asked gingerly when Ntale returned home.

"I am a bit tired," he replied dismissively. "We shall talk about that tomorrow."

It wasn't until three days later that he finally opened up and told her what he had done.

She was livid. "It's one thing being married to a poor man," she shot back, "and it's another being married to a stupid man. I tolerated the first, I can't stand the second."

She packed her belongings and left.

When I met Ntale several years after that incident, he was driving a nice car and had two houses in the suburbs of Kampala city. His children were well housed and went to good schools. His wife had returned a few weeks after she left. By Ugandan standards, they were a family living in abundance.

Incredibly, the piece of land which he had forfeited through obedience to God remained unsold for a few more years until he bought it; not as his lifeline this time, but as an addition to several other acres he had acquired by then.

"What I gave up that day wasn't just money," Ntale told me.

"It was my life, my dreams, my aspirations, it was my Isaac. If I could surrender that 400,000 shillings, there is nothing I cannot give if God asks me to."

It's almost like he died to wealth that day. He can become very rich and still not be the rich man. He fully lives a life of sowing and reaping and loves it all the way.

He got an immunization shot against the rich man virus on the day that he surrendered his livelihood in the midst an inferno of poverty. As long as he continues in a lifestyle of sowing and reaping, he cannot develop an inordinate attachment to wealth. Every act of giving is another immunization shot against the rich man virus.

Do not judge anyone but yourself

The purpose of this book is not to make you think of wealth as a dubious honor or an added temptation. Wealth belongs to God, *"who gives us richly all things **to enjoy**"* (1Tim 6:17). He wants to give riches to his children to enjoy it (!) as long as He still has their hearts.

As you might have noticed, I am emphasizing the word 'enjoy' because there are some well-meaning people who, in their overzealous efforts to collect funds for noble causes, have tended to make targeted donors feel guilty about their comfort.

"Children are dying of preventable causes while Canadians are busy enjoying their cappuccinos," wrote one concerned Canadian in a commentary that was carried in a Ugandan newspaper. While I couldn't fault the columnist for passion, I do not believe that anybody should be generous out of guilt. Canadians or whoever do not owe us a living.

The Bible says in the very next verse in First Timothy that those who are rich should be ready to give and willing to share. But having done that — and God knows so many have given generously — they should enjoy their wealth. Nobody should feel guilty about sipping a nice frothy cappuccino just because children are starving somewhere in the world. In any case Jesus said that: *"the poor people you have with you always"* (John 12:8).

Remember the context in which he said that?

He spoke those words when a perfume worth nearly a year's wages was being lavished on Him. Someone with a wrong attitude was trying to throw the 'poor people' excuse at Him to make Jesus feel guilty. Our call is to give where we are led, alleviate what we can but not to carry the weight of the world on our shoulders because none of us is God.

Then there are all those websites dedicated to casting a dark shadow on all rich preachers who have the nerve to enjoy their wealth. They front theories, attach price tags to everything the preachers own, way down to their suits, and use phrases like 'tax-exempt' and 'poor people of the world' to portray prosperous preachers as charlatans.

The media is awash with such conspiracies. Because they never seem to have any evidence of wrongdoing against the preachers, they use impressions. I practiced journalism for more than a decade so I know all about agendas. A media house will run a massive headline stating that a certain ministry is being investigated by tax authorities but will conveniently go silent when the investigation clears the ministry. In the court of public opinion — in which the media are both the prosecutor and the judge — suspicion of guilt carries nearly the same sentence as guilt.

It's to be expected for the secular media to think that a good preacher is a poor one because they do not know and don't want to know what the Bible teaches about wealth.

What astounds me is when that same resentment towards wealthy men of God comes from Christians who read the Bible. Why would anyone get angry over a preacher's lavish mansion?

Paul says that God gives us riches to enjoy (what father wouldn't want that for his children?).

Wealth is on the earth to stay. It's not going back to God. There's a lot more where He lives.

So if the children of God don't possess it, the wicked will. There is no third alternative.

I often ask Christians who get goaded when they see a wealthy preacher: Would you rather that money was spent in brothels? Do you prefer it was spent by devil worshippers?

One way or another, the wealth is here and it has to be spent by one group or the other.

Would you rather see wealth in the hands Abraham or Abimelech?

When Jacob is enriched Laban is depleted.

So would you rather see wealth with Jacob or with Laban?

Would you rather see it with Israel or with Egypt?

There's no doubt where God would rather see the wealth.

It's no wonder that when Jesus had an expensive perfume

lavished on him the first voice of indignation came from one of His own disciples.

"Why waste this?" Judas Iscariot said.

"Why was this fragrant oil not sold… and the money given to the poor?"

Does Judas care about the poor more than Jesus?

Of course he doesn't. He is just using them as a cover up for his darkest of motives.

Similarly, people who use the poor to malign servants of God who are enjoying their wealth do not care about the poor more than the people they criticize. They just use them as a cover up of their real motives. They are stricken by the Judas Iscariot spirit.

Consider the story of Francis Ntale. If you met him a few years from now living in opulent splendor it would be easy to condemn him for living such a life when 'there are poor people out there'. But you wouldn't know half the story. The man knows all about the poor; he was one of them, the worst of them. But he got out of it by obeying God in the hardest of times. How many people would do what he did?

The poor people they use to pile guilt on others are probably living in disobedience. If they were willing and obedient they too would eat the good of the land (Isa 1:19). God is no respecter of persons. You will understand this point better when you read the next chapter.

So when I read about a television preacher who bought an antic commode for $23,000 (whether or not the story is true), my reaction was not one of indignation like Judas, but one of joy like King David who said: "Let the Lord be magnified, Who has pleasure in the prosperity of His servant." (Psalms 35:27)

Staying on top of mammon

Remember, money is a good servant but a terrible master. But it is never content remaining as a servant; it wants to be the master. It's always plotting for the throne of a man's heart. But the child of God has to keep money subdued and in continual servitude.

Here are some of the practical ways of doing so.

a) What's your motive?

Our generation has mustered the art of doing the right things for the wrong reasons. Even the most self-aggrandizing and attention-seeking actions are clothed in nobility and marketed as philanthropy. Unfortunately, this sort of puffery has extended to the church.

All Christians, not just those in ministry, are called to live their lives for the audience of One.

The Apostle Paul says: *"...Do I seek to please men? For if I still pleased men, I would not be a bondservant of Christ."* (Gal 1:10)

He also tells Timothy that: *"No one engaged in warfare entangles himself with the affairs of this life that he may please him who enlisted him."* (2Tim 2:4)

I have learnt that people who get drawn into auditioning for acceptance by fellow men and striving for what the world calls 'success' can easily go down the treacherous path of the rich man virus. I have also leant that your motive will soon become your motivation.

Doctor Frank is a gynecologist who works in Kampala. As a Christian starting out his practice, he set out to be the best he could and celebrated every baby born under his watch like it was his own. He soon became popular with expecting mothers because they knew he truly cared about their wellbeing. He prayed before he embarked on any delivery and thanked God for every healthy mother and child discharged from his antenatal hospital.

Dr Frank's popularity also paid handsomely as his hospital was always busy. He bought a prime piece of land in a posh neighborhood and starting building his dream house. At about the same time he took a bank loan and bought a commercial structure in his home town. The pressure of an incomplete house and a bank loan soon took their toll on Dr Frank.

His attitude towards expecting mothers changed over time. Where he once saw them as delicate people deserving of utmost care, he now saw them as paying clients. Slowly but steadily money had become the primary motive for his practice.

He'd heard his friends say: "It's nothing personal, just business."

And that became his mantra too.

Before long Dr Frank was scheduling women for C-section who could have given birth normally and preferred to do so. Several mothers were sent to the theatre protesting, all because Caesarean births are charged nearly five times more and Dr Frank needed the money.

A lady giving birth to her third child at the same hospital noticed that the doctor no longer said a prayer before delivery and showed no emotion after the child was born.

"You must clear all dues before you are allowed to leave," was all he said as he threw off his gloves and overcoat and stormed out of the room. That was unlike the Dr Frank she once knew.

A few years later Dr Frank told his friends that he had lost interest in gynecological work. He wanted to venture into trading.

He recalled with nostalgia the days when he looked forward to seeing the next healthy baby born. What became of that passion? But there was more to it than loss of interest. His apathetic attitude had been noticed by his clients and what was once a stream of them had reduced to a trickle. His employees had often gone unpaid as money was mindlessly diverted to his numerous business misadventures. They too were resigning at an alarming rate. How did it come to that?

The Apostle Paul wrote to the Colossians and said: *"Bondservants (or employees) obey in all things your masters* (or bosses) *according to the flesh, not with eyeservice, as men-pleasers, but in sincerity of heart, fearing God. **And whatever you do, do it heartily as to the Lord and not to men."** (Col 3:22, 23). Emphasis and additions are mine.

Never let money be the primary motive for ANYTHING you do. Not even your job!

Whatever it is you do for a living; doctor, lawyer, journalist, janitor, soldier, businessman, do it heartily 'as to the Lord.'

Remember, your motive will determine your motivation.

If you do it as to the Lord like the Apostle says you will never run out of motivation. There will always be a fresh stream of grace and joy for each day. Dr Frank lost all the joy and fervor for his work the moment his motive shifted to money. If only he had heeded the Psalmist's warning that: "When riches increase do not set your heart on them."

Mammon is a terrible master. Once he takes control he starts setting up fresh targets for his captives for which they must sacrifice their principles or morals.

At the start of his practice Dr Frank never imagined that he could one day forcefully commit mothers to Caesarean births as a way of fleecing them. He had heard stories about other gynecologists doing it and wondered how they could be so horrendous. It's amazing how quickly perspectives change when money becomes the primary motive. What was once horrendous soon becomes shrewdness when seen through the prism of avarice. There is nothing one cannot do when mammon takes control. Nothing!

Even the most mundane work can be a source of continual excitement if it is done "as to the Lord." By the same token, even the most naturally exciting job can become dull and onerous if it is done to please men or, worse, as a service to mammon.

The Hebrew midwives in the first chapter of Exodus refused to listen to Pharaoh when he told them to kill the male children of Israel because "they feared God". They did their work "as to the Lord", that's why they could afford to disobey the king, and the Bible says God dealt well with the midwives.

Paul says in the very next verse in Colossians that *"knowing that from the Lord you will receive the reward of the inheritance; for you serve the Lord Christ."*

My kid sister Maria does procurement work for a company that buys different components from all across the world. She would often spot an anomaly somewhere along the procurement chain, rectify it and save the company up to $200,000 and yet someone else would take all the credit. There was this man in India who was particularly good at taking credit for work he hadn't done. What's worse is that the bosses always believed him. So Maria was slowly descending into apathy. "What's the point in working hard to save the company money when some bloke across the world is going to get all the plaudits?"

I told her to work "as to the Lord" because it is from Him that she will get a reward. She later made the biggest saving in the company in a financial year and nobody could take the credit this time. She got her big promotion.

I guess we all must choose at some stage of our lives if we want to please men or God. Those who choose to please men must then expect their reward from men. But God's reward is both guaranteed and eternal; it brings promotion in the life that now is but also earns marks for the life hereafter.

b) God is your source

It's a snare especially for people in ministry to start looking at people as their source of income.

Ministries need money to operate and God uses people to bring that money. But it's imperative that the minister never sees the people as his source otherwise he will eventually start bending to their whims.

Partners aren't always easy people to deal with. In the system of the world "he who pays the piper calls the tune". And some partners will come with the same attitude expecting that their generous contribution should give them an equally generous say in the running of the ministry.

No matter how well-meaning such partners are (many indeed mean well) they are a danger not just to the ministry and the minister but also to themselves.

They are a danger to the ministry because they often demand for special recognition in line with their carnal desires. Some ministers are tempted to put such generous contributors on the board of eldership ignoring Paul's warning that deacons and elders must not be self-willed or novices but must first be tested before they are entrusted with such positions. Any minister who does so is beginning to look at men as his source.

If God is your source, as He should be, then it's Him you must please. If a man or men are your source, then it's them you work for because your source is your boss.

The fear of man brings a snare, but whoever leans on, trusts in, and puts his confidence in the Lord is safe and set on high (Proverbs 29:25, AMP).

But partners who give generously and expect special favors are mostly a danger to themselves. Firstly, because they give with a wrong attitude and so they might not reap a financial harvest. But they will hardly concern themselves with that because they know their money bought them status in the ministry. If their attitude remains unchecked they grow to despise the hierarchy of God. The first person they despise is the pastor or minister whose arm they twisted with an offering. And so the one person who could help build them up in the faith has surrendered his authority to do so. In the end the believer is not helped.

If however a minister resolutely decides that God is his source, he will never surrender his spiritual authority to appease a generous but carnal believer.

c) Is your purpose eternal?

"If in this life only we have hope in Christ, we are of all men the most pitiable." (1Cor 15:19)

Paul is one of the people who had a tough assignment. Jesus said of him: *"For I will show him how many things he must suffer for my name's sake."* (Acts 9:16)

So if our story ended when we died, then Paul would indeed be the most pitiable of men. He would have wasted his life. "I have fought with beasts at Ephesus, what advantage is it for me?" he asked. Why would he have suffered so much if it ended here?

Even God's justice system looks flawed if you look at it from an earthly perspective. The early Christians were fed to lions for professing Christ while we can profess Him on television, radio and all media platforms, even on our cars with stickers and nobody is going to feed us to lions. Ezekiel had to lie on his side for 430 days while Solomon lived in splendor all his days. None of that would make sense if it ended here.

Of course it does not end here. Believers open themselves

up to deception, especially in the area of money, when they lose sight of the eternal purpose of God. Everything God does has an eternal purpose, and so should everything we do.

"And you shall remember the Lord your God for it is He who gives you power to get wealth, that He may establish His covenant which He swore to your fathers, as it is this day." (Deut 8:18)

God's perspective even of wealth is eternal. Even if "we brought nothing into this world and it is certain we can carry nothing out", we can use the wealth herein to serve God and fulfill his eternal purpose; which is salvation for mankind.

People who lose sight of that eternal purpose eventually adopt the worldly view of success and start looking at wealth as an end in itself, rather than as a means to an end. That makes them susceptible to the rich man virus.

Chapter 6

Giving end or receiving end?

But a generous man devises generous things, and by generosity he shall stand. (Isaiah 32:8)

Generosity starts as a choice, then it grows into a habit and finally it becomes a part of someone's personality. Those who practice generosity live by it.

Habitual givers get consumed by their giving and always seem to have something extra to give. They are often on the lookout for someone to help or a cause to support.

They don't give because they can afford to. They do it out of habit. In fact they often give when they can ill afford to, but it's almost like they cannot help themselves. Consequently, they

The Rich Man Virus

develop an abundance mentality which produces perpetual abundance.

Since their tendency is to solve problems, habitual givers are often inventive, ingenious and farsighted. They have a mindset that is engineered to creating solutions. They are more likely to be innovators or entrepreneurs.

They are the sons of Jacob.

However, for every giver there is a receiver. For every benefactor there is a beneficiary.

By the same token, receiving starts as a preference then grows into a habit and finally becomes a part of someone's personality. Habitual receivers are just as consumed with receiving as givers are with giving. Consequently, they never seem to have enough. They develop a lack mentality and are perpetually needy; always on the lookout for aid. No amount of help can cure their state.

Receivers convince themselves that givers give because they can afford to. They believe that they would be just as generous if they had as much. That, of course, is a lie; for more reasons than one.

Firstly, because generosity is not a statement of plenty. It's a choice, a habit, then a personality trait.

Secondly, receivers will never experience abundance. That's because abundance is firstly a mindset before it is actualized in three-dimensional reality. Only those who proactively practice abundance before they experience it will experience it.

Habitual receivers tend to be unimaginative. They are often self-occupied and nearsighted.

Giving end or receiving end?

They have an eye trained to see problems and not solutions. They believe that their contribution to society is to spot what's wrong. That's as far as their effort goes.

They are the sons of Esau

These are two distinct groups of people that can scarcely mix. You are either on the giving side or on the receiving side of life. There are no in-betweens.

Jacob I loved, Esau I hated

People on the giving end of life find it natural to be forward-thinking and make decisions in the present that will make them comfortable in the future. By contrast, those on the receiving end live for the moment, enjoying every bit of gratification as and when it comes.

The contrast of personalities between Jacob and Esau, the twin sons of Isaac, is as intriguing as any in the Bible.

Jacob was a fighter literary from his birth. Yet as an adult he was mild (which literary means complete according to the New King James). He spent most of his time in his tent. He was deep and introspective. More importantly, Jacob was a forward thinker, he thought generationally. That's why he valued the blessing over the substance; a fact that was illustrated so many times in his life. He lived on the giving side of life.

Esau on the other hand was an outdoors man; a skilled hunter who spent most of his time on the move. He was shallow and impulsive; a man for the moment. He acted first and thought later. He sought satisfaction in the present time. The future would take care of itself.

Esau returned home one evening from his endless travels and travails to find Jacob in possession of a decent meal. Esau saw food that would solve his immediate problem while Jacob, the meditative and perceptive schemer, saw an opportunity, not just of a lifetime but of generations.

Imagine the difference in perspective!

Knowing the impulsive nature of his brother, Jacob made his indecent proposal. His heart must have been pounding when he suggested to his brother an exchange that would see him run off with a generational blessing in exchange for a plate of food.

But Esau, as nearsighted and flippant as ever, said: *"Look I am about to die so what is this birthright to me?"*

Esau realized much later that he had been conned of something so valuable when he arrived too late to claim his firstborn convocation from their ageing father.

"I have blessed Jacob and indeed he shall be blessed," Isaac told Esau. "I have made him your master."

Esau cried bitterly and said: "Have you not reserved a blessing for me… have you only one blessing?"

Regret is the inevitable destination for habitual receivers. Like Esau, who thought he could eat the food and take the blessing too, habitual receivers think they can beat the system and wind up as double beneficiaries. They are deluded.

Receivers look out for the substance but givers prefer the blessing. Those who choose to live on the giving end will always be superior to those who receive because Jesus said: *"It's more blessed to give than to receive."* (Acts 20:35)

Giving end or receiving end?

The contrast in character between these twins doesn't stop at that.

Jacob was a man for delayed gratification. He refused to take a wife from the Canaanites among whom they lived and was well into his 40s when he got his first wife from among his mother's relatives in Padan Aram. But Esau, a man for the momentary high, was already enjoying the company of his two Hittite wives, whom the Bible says *"were a grief of mind to Isaac and Rebekah (his parents)."* (Gen 26:34-35)

Esau, being the typical reactionary, realized belatedly that his choice of wives had lost him favor with his parents. So he went and got a third wife from one of Abraham's grandchildren through Ishmael.

Jacob was always ahead of the game.

Jacob was a visionary. As soon as he had received the blessing, he left his rich father's house with all the inheritance and ran away with nothing but a staff. How bold is that? When God appeared to him at Bethel, Jacob vowed that he would give a tithe of whatever substance he acquired on his journey. Even when he had nothing to give, he was a giver.

While Jacob had to work 20 years for a charlatan in order to earn his own wealth, I suppose all the wealth of Isaac was passed on to Esau, who gleefully received it.

When Laban, Jacob's uncle for whom he worked, sought to tie him down with a salary that would probably guarantee his servitude for life, Jacob wisely turned it down and came up with something so ingenious.

So he (Laban) said: "What shall I give you?"

And Jacob said: "You shall not give me anything. If you will do this thing for me, I will again feed and keep your flocks."

"Let me pass through all your flock today, removing from there all the **speckled and spotted sheep**, *and all the* **brown ones among the lambs**, *and the* **spotted and speckled among the goats;** *and* **these shall be my wages.** *So my righteousness will answer for me in time to come, when the subject of my wages comes before you: every one that is not speckled and spotted among the goats, and brown among the lambs, will be considered stolen, if it is with me."*

From the natural perspective, Jacob had shot himself in the foot. How often will you see speckled and spotted sheep? They must have been very few if any among the flock. No wonder Laban was excited over his son-in-law's apparent foolishness, and said: "Oh that it were according to your word."

Through some bit of God-inspired ingenuity, Jacob turned the best of Laban's flock into his own and acquired a great deal of wealth. People who choose to live on the giving end of life are often more creative.

Having acquired a great deal of wealth, Jacob's biggest trial came when he had to meet his brother on his return to Canaan. He trembled when he heard that Esau was moving towards him. But Jacob knew that his brother had a weakness for receiving, so he said: *"I will appease him with the present that goes before me and afterward I will see his face..."* (Gen 32:20)

How derisory is that? Having stolen Esau's generational blessing, Jacob said: (I paraphrase) "I know my brother, he is a habitual receiver, I will just send him a few cattle and sheep and he will have calmed himself down by the time we meet."

And that's precisely how it punned out. Even if Esau put up a show of refusing the gift from his brother, he eventually took it (Gen 33:11).

Earlier on, Jacob had done something else that demonstrated his extraordinary attitude. He sent all his company; his two wives, children and all his substance across the brook into the hands of a hostile brother. Then he stayed alone overnight and fought with God for a blessing. He risked his labor of 20 years to wrestle for some more blessing. That's a man on the giving end of life. That day he had his name changed to Israel.

I suppose that's why the scripture says "Jacob I have loved, but Esau I have hated."

It's not so much the person that God loves (chooses) or hates (rejects) but the personalities. Jacob valued intangibles over tangibles. He valued the blessing, which lasts for generations, while Esau his brother couldn't look beyond the present.

"...while we do not look at the things which are seen, but at the things which are not seen. For the things which are seen are temporary, but the things which are not seen are eternal." (2 Cor 4:18:)

Jacob valued the unseen things which are eternal over the temporary tangibles. He is the godfather of all the people who live on the giving end.

Too poor to give?

Those who live on the receiving end of life soon develop a dependency mindset. The only creativity they are capable of is geared towards squeezing more aid out of their benefactors. I have seen some people go down that road and never extricate themselves.

Eventually they start thinking of their dependency as some sort of skill that they alone possess. At that point they no longer think of their helpers as kind-hearted or generous but as foolish and gullible.

They never stop to wonder why the gullible givers always have an abundance and why they, the wise and crafty receivers, are always in more desperate need. At that point of decay, the kindest thing the benefactor can do is cut off the supply because every extra aid simply pushes the beneficiary deeper into the abyss.

That's a very sorry state for anyone to find themselves in; a state in which the only way they can be helped is by not being helped.

As the decaying process continues, receivers start to see themselves as deserving of everything they get. Even their tones change. They no longer ask for aid, they demand for it.

If you want to see what's in the heart of a habitual receiver dare to cut off the supply chain. You will be shocked when the words of entreaty previously used are replaced with abusive rhetoric.

I do not believe that God intended for any one group of people to supply while another continuously consumes.

"For I do not mean that others should be eased and you burdened." (2Cor 8:13)

It is pointless continuing to give to someone who will not also give. In the end, neither party is helped. It might be good for the ego of the giver to know that there's someone down the food chain who is dependent on him or her, but there's no blessing in that.

"We want to tell you further, brethren, about the grace of God which has been evident in the churches of Macedonia. For in the midst of an ordeal of severe tribulation, **their depth of poverty has overflowed in lavish generosity** *on their part.* (2Cor 8:1-4, AMP)

For, as I can bear witness, [they gave] according to their ability, yes, and beyond their ability; and [they did it] voluntarily…

No one is too destitute to give. Notice that the Macedonian churches, in spite of their deep poverty, pleaded with the apostles to receive their gift. They were generous when they clearly couldn't afford to be. And they did it voluntarily without any compulsion.

I have seen people who gave their way out of poverty but I am yet to meet someone who received his or her way out of destitution. Not one!

Not a person. Not a nation.

The receiving end syndrome is progressive. Eventually receivers drop all pretensions of self-reliance and settle indolently for a lifetime of dependency. They sacrifice their creative genius at the altar of aid.

Curious case of Ethiopia

In the early 1980s, Ethiopia was inundated by the two cataclysms that are civil war and drought. Either one of them can cause a major catastrophe in the precarious Horn of Africa nation; a combination of the two caused devastation of truly earth-shattering proportions.

By 1983, reports of an impending food shortage in Ethiopia were featuring sporadically in the world media. But it wasn't until early 1985 that the devastation was played out to the disbelieving world through graphically alarming pictures on television and in print.

A group of pop star musicians were shocked into action and, within a few months, collected about $230m for the starving people of Ethiopia through a hit song they performed jointly. The awareness they created led to a lot more money being collected from various sources. The immediate danger was soon averted, but not before one million people had died of starvation and hunger-related illnesses.

But the generosity of the world, even if it saved lives, created an intrinsic problem for the people of that country. Ethiopians didn't seem to mind being the objects of world pity. The cash raked in wasn't bad either.

Close to three decades later, Ethiopia has yet to be weaned off food aid. What was a situational problem in the early and mid 1980s has now become generational problem. Several famines have been reported in Ethiopia since then, the most recent is ongoing even as I write this, and more pleas for aid have gone out. In 2009, the country received in excess of $500m in food aid from World Food Program alone. And there's no shortage of other aid agencies pressing the same soft spot, using well-rehearsed reminders of the 1985 disaster to coerce donors to dig deeper into their (recently) recession-hit pockets. The trouble with such dependency is that generations of Ethiopians will be raised into believing that the world owes them a good meal.

Imagine what damage that does to their creativity. If necessity is the mother of invention, then what sort of creativity is possible from people whose most basic need is met by other people?

Yet Ethiopia is no barren country. On the contrary, it is reasonably green and very well watered. Much of the country is blessed with rich soils and it has one of the most rivers in the world. Over 85% of the total River Nile water flow comes from Ethiopia.

The Horn of Africa country is also a sporting powerhouse which churns out middle and long distance athletes off a seemingly endless conveyer belt. What's more, it has enough natural features to become a big tourism earner. In fact it has the largest number of UNESCO World Heritage sites in Africa.

So why would such a country be in constant peril, one delayed rainy season away from a devastating famine? Because of being on the receiving end!

If Ethiopians stopped thinking of themselves as perpetual victims they could easily become a regional food basket. They would revise their land tenure system to allow for mechanized commercial agriculture and would use their many rivers to irrigate the crop and cut their dependence on rainy seasons. Then they could easily be supplying much-needed food to neighboring Somalia which is almost entirely covered by desert and at least has an admissible excuse for depending on World Food Program handouts.

That's true not just for Ethiopia but for so many other African countries which are far too comfortable receiving millions of dollars in aid to worry about self-reliance.

In October 2011 the Ugandan president went and did something very unthinkable in the eyes of his people; he donated $5.5m to schools in Burundi.

"Burundi is a poor country which is recovering from war," the president explained. "I am therefore of the opinion that where we can, we should support them."

But few people, if any, shared his view. Ugandans were seething with rage because the timing of the donation was ironic, to say the least. It came at a time when Uganda's teachers were threatening to go on strike over poor pay. Media critics wrote scathing opinions slating the president's 'cowboy generosity' at a time when we could ill afford it. Their columns were reflective of the general public mood.

The Secretary to the Treasury, the man who had signed off the donation, was called to appear before the Parliamentary Public Accounts Committee to explain the decision. A bewildered committee chairman asked him: "Is your heart in Kampala or in Bujumbura (the Burundi capital)?"

"How can you donate all this money to Burundi schools when our children studying in Universal Primary Education schools are suffering? Are you really a Ugandan?"

As the debate raged on — and it did for weeks — Ugandan newspapers reported in a matter-of-fact way that the European Union, in spite of its own growing crisis and the threat of a Euro Zone collapse, had donated tens of millions of Euros to the Ugandan education sector. That, of course, was in addition to the millions they had already given in budget support and for many other causes. That story was consigned to the inner pages because the more prominent space was still being used to express fury from all quarters over the president's donation to Burundi. Yet none of the erudite media critics saw any irony in that.

We have no problem with generosity as long as we are on the receiving end. But on those rare occasions when our country gives those who are worse off than we are it attracts a parliamentary probe.

I am not ignorant of the fact that big-nation donations to countries like Uganda are not born purely out of good-natured generosity — it's a lot more complex than that — but they give; and we receive. As long as it stays that way so will the status quo. Jesus said it's more blessed to give than to receive.

The sad reality is that many African countries have gone down the tunnel of receiving-end decay and have arrived at the point where no amount of aid can turn them around. The only thing that could help them is a change in disposition from perpetual beneficiaries to benefactors. It's amazing how transformational a simple shift of mindset can be. All it would take to spark the creative genius that has been lying idle for over a century is for Africans to stop seeing themselves as problem nations and start thinking of themselves as problem solvers. Only then can they see the wealth that God has deposited above and below the soils of this continent.

The receiving-end syndrome has the ability to cripple individuals, communities, nations and even a continent. People suffering from it are blind to resources and deaf to possibilities. All they see are insurmountable hurdles. Therefore they become bland, unimaginative and are natural short-term thinkers.

So are you living on the giving end or on the receiving end?

Chapter 7

Peddlers of the word

*For we are not, **as so many, peddling the word of God;** but as of sincerity, but as from God, we speak in the sight of God in Christ.* (2Cor 2:17:)

Paul says that he and his co-minister Timothy are not like many others who are peddling the word of God. In the cross references of the New King James translation, peddling is described as adulterating for gain. The Amplified Bible says "we are not like hucksters, making a trade of the word of God, adulterating or shortchanging it."

It's interesting to note that people who corrupted and made a trade of the word of God for dishonest gain existed as far back as Paul's time. These are businessmen whose commodity is the word of God. Paul says that these peddlers of the word are "so many". If that was true in the early days of the gospel, imagine how much truer it is today.

Around the mid 1990s some friends of mine organized a week-long Bible teaching conference at a church in one of the outskirts of Kampala city and I was invited to preach on Friday. There was such a palpable hunger for God in those days and the Holy Spirit always responded to it. People got healed and baptized in the Holy Spirit as the crowd simply worshipped and basked in the presence of God. The pastor of the church came around a bit later in the evening. He walked through the auditorium and went straight into his office just behind the pulpit area. As the service drew to a close I took an offering and closed my eyes to pray over it. But when I opened my eyes the baskets had vanished. For a moment I was in shock but I looked to my left and saw two ushers disappearing into the pastor's office with them. The episode was like a scene out of a comedy and my friends and I had a nice laugh over it. One of them playfully suggested that since I had asked God to "accept the offerings" I must have thought He had done so more literally than I bargained for.

The pastor was a diminutive and reticent man always welcomed visiting preachers. He was marching to his van when I stopped him and I tried to get him into a conversation. But he was uptight and gave the impression that he would rather be on his way.

I got to know later that his attitude was a protective mask because he expected the subject of the collection to be raised. But I had other things on my mind. I was bubbling with excitement over the wonderful things God had done in the service. His indifference shocked me. Nonetheless, I blubbered on like a kid narrating the exploits of his favorite cartoon character to his pensive father who can't wait to get back to his newspaper. He must have marveled at my naivety.

Few people who heard our story were surprised. That pastor's reputation in the area of church finance was, to put it mildly, far from impeccable. He ran a number of businesses in town and to him the church was nothing more than an extension of his enterprises. He passed by after every service to balance books and carry off whatever collection was left.

No wonder he seemed so disinterested in my Holy Spirit rhetoric.

His congregation got to know about his ways with money and the collection dwindled steadily. That's why he was hospitable to visiting preachers; they guaranteed a bigger offering. That was the last time I interacted with him.

I drove by that neighborhood several years later and noticed that a block of shops stood where the church once was. The ministry had folded, the congregation scattered and the pastor had gone into fulltime trading. I can't say I was surprised. He is not the only pastor or preacher whose ministry has been destroyed through the stealth operations of mammon.

I quote from Kenneth E. Hagin's book *"He gave gifts unto men"*.

"Over the years, I have sometimes seen people use their ministries and the anointing that is upon them to obtain money from people. For example, I once visited a certain minister's meetings, who had a marvelous healing ministry. In this particular meeting, five deaf and mute people were brought from the state institution to be healed. This man ministered to all five of these men, and they were all instantly healed and could both hear and speak.

Immediately, the minister stopped the meeting and began taking up an offering. He knew he would be able to get a large offering because of the mighty demonstration of God's power. People from all over the meeting ran to give him money because of these miraculous healings. This man used his ministry and, really, the healing power of God to obtain money in a wrong way. What happened to this minister? This character weakness, as well as other faults he didn't correct, eventually cost him not only his ministry, but his life.

In the first vision when Jesus appeared to me in Rockwall, Texas, one of the things He said to me was, "There are two things to be careful of. Number one, be sure you always give all the honor and the glory for everything that happens unto Me and unto My Name.

"Secondly, be very careful about money. Many on whom I've placed My Spirit and called unto such a ministry and anointed have become money-minded and have lost the anointing."

The more people get attached to money the colder they grow towards God. That's a given.

I have showed you in previous chapters how mammon destroys his victims. Sadly, some of those victims were anointed ministers who started off well-intentioned but swallowed the first seemingly innocuous bait. Before they knew it, they had lost control and were sliding inexorably down the destructive path of greed and avarice.

If the junkie lying inebriated at the roadside knew where he would end up, he wouldn't have taken that curiosity-driven first shot of cocaine. If Judas Iscariot knew that he would end up hanging on a tree with his intestines spilled out he wouldn't have dipped his finger into the money bag that first time.

I recall a time so many years ago when army recruiters came to my home town. Many youth my age went to the ground where the exercise was carried out, some to enlist but many others as curious spectators.

The requirements were easy; a health checkup and a letter from your village chief. The young men and women who had successfully enlisted were taken to the side, given snacks and generally treated like VIPs in full view of everyone. They looked so enviable. So the queues built up as more youths were tempted to join that preferred group. The process ended when the recruiting officers decided they had enough people, even if many more were still in queue.

That's when the recruits were given a taste of what lay ahead. The officer in charge told them that freedom, as they once knew it, ended that moment. Now they had to do only as they are told. They were frog-marched and taken through a humbling exercise meant to break their wills before being bundled onto a waiting bus like convicts. The sudden shift from

VIP treatment to torture shocked many of them out of their wild fantasies. Some tried to change their minds but were curtly told that it was too late. As the bus drove off, the youths who had missed out were glad they had arrived late for the exercise.

If those recruits had known what lay ahead, many of them wouldn't have enlisted.

Any preacher who steps into the world of craft or manipulation to raise money might similarly lose control over the outcome — I know many who have — and before they know it, they are recruits in the army of mammon and are being kicked and frog-marched by their new master to the shock of onlookers.

Not all that glitters

A church I once attended welcomed a visiting preacher some years ago and what a stir he caused. He was short, portly, very smart and such a smooth talker. He spoke on the subject of 'giving up your Isaac'. I could tell from the start that he was a master of his craft.

Clearly, it was a message he had preached several times over. It rolled off his tongue with the fluidity of a news anchor reading off a teleprompter. He described King Solomon's massive sacrifice at the opening of the temple in such graphic detail it sent our imaginations into overdrive.

"Imagine a flock of 100 bulls," he said in a feline tone meant to capture our imagination.

"Now imagine a thousand bulls."

And so we did.

"Alright, now imagine twenty-two thousand bulls being slaughtered one after the other" he said broodingly, using appropriate gesticulations to help our already stretched imagination.

By the time he got to the one hundred and twenty thousand sheep that were also sacrificed that day, the entirety of our bank accounts looked like the widow's two pence in comparison. He seasoned his message with dramatic testimonies of people who had surrendered their most valued possessions and seen tremendous financial miracles.

When he called for people to give their 'Isaac', very few stayed in their seats. He called them to the pulpit and, one by one, they announced on the microphone what exactly they were going to give. I witnessed the whole drama pensively from my seat.

In my mind, he was just another peddler of the word.

Peddlers of the word are often terrific public speakers with an exceptional knowledge of the part of scripture that suits their trade. They have mustered the art of arousing emotions. Their choice of words and intonations are calculated to indulge the fancy of their listeners. They use craft to break into the imagination of the congregation and take it through a rollercoaster of emotions. Many of the testimonies they give are either plain lies or gross exaggerations. It's all part of the business.

The trouble for Christendom is that peddlers of the word cannot easily be told apart from genuine prosperity preachers. The principles they teach are right, and so are the Biblical references they use. But their motives are all wrong. Many of them started off genuine but were tempted just that once to step away from faith and into craft. The first time wasn't easy.

A pastor friend of mine told me about the first time he attempted craft because he had seen other people do it and appear to prosper. He preached a Holy Spirit inspired message and stopped right at the peak of it and asked the church to "come and sow into this anointing".

The congregation responded enthusiastically but his inner man flushed a clear red light.

"I felt so bad, it was like the Holy Spirit had lifted off me," he said.

He went back to his room, repented and has since watched his motives.

The rich man virus is easy to snuff out at the start; before it takes root. The only difference between it and a biological virus is that the rich man virus eats the God-loving cells not the body cells.

That pastor didn't have to respond that way. He could just as easily have ignored the voice of his spirit and carried on with the vice. Soon the inner voice would be sufficiently subdued and he would proceed to enjoy the fruits of his craft. That's what so many other preachers do — according to Apostle Paul's estimation, not mine.

Peddlers of the word do not stop at using words; they employ all manner of tactics which are intended to compel people to give a bigger offering. Even if the compulsion is soft, it exerts meaningful pressure. But in his letter to Philemon, Paul said: *".... in order that your benevolence might not seem to be the result of compulsion or of pressure but might be voluntary [on your part].* (V14 AMP)

Paul also says: "Let each one [give] as he has made up his own mind and purposed in his heart, not reluctantly or sorrowfully or under compulsion…" (2Cor 9:7)

That man from my story called people to give their 'Isaac' and gave them a microphone to blot it out to the entire church. That's an ingenious thing to do when you want money, and I saw the evidence of it that day.

The first person speaks out and says that he is giving half a million. The congregation claps. The next person is tempted to give a million. The cheer is louder. Then two million, and the graph rises. Nobody wants to spoil the party by giving less than the previous person. By the end of the exercise people had surrendered their cars for the momentary gratification of a louder cheer.

Any form of giving that appeals to people's carnal desire to be recognized is fundraising, not Biblical sowing. People who give with such a motive will not reap.

But a peddler is not bothered if people get the promised harvest or not. All he cares for are the wares. I am told that that preacher returned the following week and forcefully demanded for every penny of the offering. After a big quarrel with the pastor, he carried off everything that had been gathered and moved on to his next destination.

Some peddlers have convinced themselves that there is nothing wrong with what they do. Many others know that there is everything wrong with it, but they justify it with statements like "the church needs the money for this project". The truth, however, is that they have stepped too deep into the mire to pull themselves out.

And yet amidst all that, there are many genuine ministers anointed to preach the gospel of prosperity. They always talk about money, sowing and reaping and can easily be mistaken for peddlers. But they are not. Even if they appear to say the same things and use the same Biblical references, the difference between genuine prosperity preachers and peddlers is distinct to the discerning observer.

While peddlers speak out of their mind to the people's minds, seeking to stir up emotions, honest prosperity preachers speak from their spirit to your spirit.

Honest prosperity preachers don't just speak the word, they live it. They are the embodiment of the sowing practice they advocate for. They speak out of conviction not convenience. It's not about what they want from you but what they want for you. Like Paul, they "do not seek the gift, but they seek the fruit that abounds to your account." (Phil 4:17)

Their message is confirmed by your inner man. They do not use soft compulsion meant to exert pressure on the giver. They do not seek to move people whom God has not moved. They preach the word and allow the Holy Spirit to move His people.

Most of the testimonies they give to backup the message are about incidences when they sowed and reaped. That's because they are on the giving end of life. And they seek to arouse a conviction in you that draws you into the habit of sowing. They are not looking for a collection for the moment but for a lifestyle of sowing. They do not glorify a big offering and belittle a small one. That's because they understand — like Jesus demonstrated — that little can be big and big can be little. And they do not employ crafty methods that flatter people and appeal to their egos to make them give more than they have purposed.

None of the New Testament preachers spoke or wrote about the subject of money, generosity and giving more than Apostle Paul. But he clearly distinguishes himself from peddlers who did it for the wrong motives when he writes that: *"For as you well know, we never resorted to words of flattery or to any cloak to conceal greedy motives or pretexts for gain, as God is our witness* (1 Thes 2:5 Amp).

Notice that the difference is not so much in the message but in the motive and method.

Peddlers will mostly give testimonies about people who sowed into their ministry and reaped big. That's because they are looking for an instant reaction. They hardly ever speak about their own giving because they hardly ever give. They ask you to give your 'Isaac' when they have never given their 'Ishmael'. They are severely afflicted with the rich man virus. They have a sense of entitlement that is ungodly. They believe the giving message was handed down for their ravenous benefit. They live on the receiving end of life.

You can tell that they are fixated on the day's collection, nothing more. If they must use trickery, flattery or lies to make it bigger, they will. They are fundraisers not prosperity teachers.

But because the church is so inundated with the practice of fundraising, these peddlers never run out of church platforms on which to practice their craft. As a matter of fact, many of them are on high demand for their ability to wring money out of congregations. Pastors or preachers who embrace such methods because they must raise money — even for noble causes — have taken a step along a notoriously slippery path.

Interestingly, I have never seen any of those peddlers living a life of abundance. They always seem to be looking for the next survival kit.

Jeremiah 48:10 says: *"Cursed is he who does the work of the Lord deceitfully."*

They may put up appearances to look prosperous and even speak ostentatiously about things they purport to own but if you dig beneath the facade you will find a miserable day-by-day existence.

People who yield to craft must then depend on it. "Do you not know that to whom you present yourselves slaves to obey, you are that one's slaves whom you obey…." (Rom 6:6)

The godfather of peddlers

There is nothing particularly new about people using the gift and platform of God for commercial purposes. The practice has existed for ages. Probably the first man to go that way was Balaam the son of Beor, who was a prophet in the days of Israel's sojourn from Egypt. He had the word of God and it was said of him that "he whom you bless is blessed and he whom you curse is cursed".

Now Balak was the king of Moab at the time and he was dreadfully scared of the children of Israel who had encamped around his country. So he sent for Balaam the prophet to curse

Israel and weaken it to the point where it could be defeated in battle.

But God told Balaam clearly that: "You shall not go with them."

But the Moabite king wasn't that easily put off. He sent for Balaam another time and added a sweetener: "I will certainly honor you greatly."

On the one hand Balaam had a clear instruction from God that he mustn't go. But the promise of honor by the king was too good to ignore. So he came up with a creative way of settling this dilemma. He spoke all the right words but disobeyed God with his actions.

He said: *"Though Balak were to give me his house full of silver and gold, I could not go beyond the word of the Lord my God, to do less or more."*

Yet he went with the messengers of the king against the instruction of God. But he also dressed that up with some powerful words: *"The word that the Lord puts in my mouth, that I must speak."*

On his way to Moab, an angel of God stood in front of him to block him. The donkey on which he rode saw the angel but Balaam didn't. Isn't that amazing? An ass being more spiritually perceptive than a prophet?

Balaam's backsliding was slow but steady. One step of disobedience led to the next. Eventually he found himself on the high places of Baal, from where he would have cursed Israel if God hadn't intervened and put words of blessing in his mouth instead.

Then Balak told him that: *"I said I would greatly honor you, but in fact, the Lord has kept you back from honor."*

Having failed to curse Israel, Balaam gave counsel to the Moabite king and told him to entice the children of Israel with women. It worked. The men of Israel gleefully descended on the Moabite women who lured them into Baal worship. Their harlotry caused a plague that killed twenty four thousand of the children of Israel.

Ultimately, Balaam, the once-mighty prophet, became an enemy to the people of God. He was killed like a common man when Israel attacked Midian and slaughtered all their men.

Balaam erred by putting his anointing and his prophetic word up for hire (Neh 13:2) and therefore he became the godfather of peddlers of the word; of all people who exchange the anointing and the word of God for wealth and honor.

Even in the early church there were ministers who similarly put their anointing up for hire. The Apostles speak about them in their epistles.

Peter says *"they have a heart trained in covetous (lustful, greedy) practices, and are accursed children. They have forsaken the right way and gone astray, following the way of Balaam the son of Beor, who loved the wages of unrighteousness."* (2Pet 2:14-15 AMP)

Jude says such ministers have *"abandoned themselves for the sake of gain, following the error of Balaam, and have perished in rebellion [like that] of Korah!* (Jude v11 AMP)

Paul also has something to say about them. He calls them people *"whose god is their belly, and whose glory is in their shame—who set their mind on earthly things."* (Phil 3:19)

Greed is greedy

The problem with greed is that it is greedy

It feeds on itself. It is never a one-off proposition. It is never satisfied.

The first step into greed is the most significant. The rest are easy.

The downslide begins when a preacher steps out of faith and steps into craft.

Faith grows and so does craft.

Paul says: *"But we have renounced the hidden things of shame, not walking in craftiness, nor handling the word of God deceitfully...."* (2Cor 4:2)

Someone who believes God for a nice meal will eventually believe God for a plush house in a rich neighborhood because "the just shall live by faith".

Similarly, anyone who uses craftiness to get a nice meal will want to use it to get a plush house in a rich neighborhood because the crafty live by craft.

One of the biggest dangers of mammon is that it clothes itself in wisdom, smartness, shrewdness or whatever other euphemism you can conjure for sneaky money grabbing. That is what makes the rich man virus so difficult to contain once it gains ground in a man's heart. People who have an inordinate love for money start to think of themselves as smarter than those who do not. That's the biggest danger.

By contrast, Christians who get entangled in sexual vice, in pornography and other forms of destructive addictions are always aware of their shortcomings and are therefore more likely to go to the cross to obtain full deliverance and reignite their fire for God.

But those caught in the swoop of mammon grow to love and cherish their weakness, not identifying it as such. For the most part they enjoy drifting downstream and don't realize that there's a steep waterfall ahead. Even if such people stay in church — and for the most part they do — their hearts are in the world. Their criterion of success is in sync with the carnal world and revolves around wanton materialism.

Naturally, the more their hearts are drawn towards the material comforts of this world, the more they are drawn away from God. *"Do not love the world or the things in the world,"* the Apostle *John writes in his first epistle. "If anyone loves the world the love of the father is not in him."*

People who get caught in the web of mammon start by losing taste for the things of God. It happens inwardly and only the most discerning observer will notice. Outwardly, nothing about them changes. Not in the short run. They continue doing the same things, quoting the same scriptures and preaching the same messages. But inwardly, everything has changed. Their priorities are being realigned away from God.

As a result of that realignment, a man or woman who used to get excited about the move of the Spirit finds that he or she is no longer enthused by it. Testimonies of healings and outpourings that once excited him suddenly sound banal. Such apathy is the earliest sign that the rich man virus has begun its work.

A few people notice that indifference towards the things of

God and move to re-ignite their fire. But many others continue with the downslide until they grow to despise the things of God.

I remember attending a prophetic conference with a preacher friend of mine not too long ago. The power of God was so evident and left virtually everyone at the meeting in awe.

But not this particular gentleman.

We were in deep thought as we walked away from the meeting and I presumed we had the same thing on our minds. That was until he broke the silence. He commented on the affluence of the congregation (I suppose he judged it from the type of cars in the parking yard) and wondered how big the offering in such a place could be.

I was flummoxed. I saw someone who had lost any sense of godly awe. Paul calls such people *"men of corrupt minds and destitute of the truth, who suppose that godliness is a means of gain." He goes on to recommend: "From such withdraw yourself."* (1 Tim 6:5)

That's precisely what I did.

Notably, that gentleman is not rich by any standards. As a matter of fact he qualifies to be called destitute. But he is afflicted by the rich man virus.

Here in a nutshell is the progression of the rich man virus.

People who catch it start by losing their sense of awe over the things of God; they are underwhelmed by the things that once excited them. Then they descend into apathy or indifference. Eventually they grow to despise the wisdom of God (especially in the area of finance) because they replace it with their own 'wisdom'.

Then they despise genuine servants of God who are living by faith not craft, even if they still operate among them.

At that stage of the downslide mammon has surrounded them and is ready for the final onslaught. He will not stop until he sits on the throne of their heart; that's where he wants to be. He is a master and demands worship. When mammon is through with his work, his victim winds up despising God.

Yet mammon does not want his converts within the church to leave the church. He prefers for them to stay and operate within church circles so they can win more converts for him. Judas Iscariot was sitting in the upper room with Jesus long after mammon had captured him.

Having accepted the inevitability of Jesus' impending death, the other disciples were captivated by His every word. Not Judas. He must have been bored rigid when Jesus was breaking bread and sharing wine with His disciples, talking to them about the new covenant. With another master sitting on the throne of his heart, he was increasingly out of place. Finally, he decided that he'd endured enough of all the spiritual gibberish and stormed out to go and cut a deal for himself with the Pharisees.

Similarly, converts of mammon stay within the church and use ostentation to draw people away from the path of faith. They are the masters of pomp, speaking *"great swelling words of emptiness, they allure through the lusts of the flesh, through lewdness, the ones who have actually escaped from those who live in error."* (2Peter 2:18)

They are ones who popularized the culture of orphanages that exist only in brochures. They prey on the kind hearts of people who want to help the needy. Then they use their ill-gotten wealth to spread the word and recruit people from faith to craft. They offer an enticing shortcut to affluence and many believers and preachers fall for it.

Remember, the godfather of peddlers Balaam wound up practicing sorcery on the high places of Baal. And it all started with a simple act of disobedience prompted by a promise of honor from a heathen king.

Ministers who are tempted into craft have two alternatives; turn back and start over or go deeper into it. But craft is not sustainable. After a while even the craftiest people lose their ability to keep people spellbound with their words. At that point they realize that they need a higher spiritual power to continue in their trade. That's when mammon makes the grand proposal, often through another minister who has sold his soul. That's how people who started out serving God with the noblest motives but allowed themselves to step into craft end up joining demonic secret societies which are rooted in devil worship. As sad a progression as that is, some people have taken it.

The case of Gehazi

It's possible for someone to be raised in the ways of God, experience some of the most awesome moves of the Spirit and stay around people who operate in the supernatural but still chose the worldly way. That's what happened to Gehazi the servant of Elisha.

He had witnessed all the miracles performed by the prophet, had seen a host of angels surrounding Dothan after his eyes were opened, and he was in line to inherit that anointing, yet

Gehazi gave it all up for two talents of silver and two changes of garments, and all because he wasn't patient enough to follow God's plan.

I am not promoting the virtues of the poor preacher espoused by religion. Neither, by the way, was Elisha.

Notice what Elisha told Gehazi after the apprentice had taken Naaman's goodies.

"**Is it time** to receive money and to receive clothing, oil groves and vineyards, sheep and oxen, male and female servants?" (2 Kings 5:26)

The key word in that passage is highlighted. Some translations say "is this the time" (NIV)

In other words, Elisha was telling Gehazi that there would come a time in future when he would have gotten all those things. He wasn't destined to be needy all his life. If he had waited a little longer, he would get not just Elisha's anointing but also all the nice things in life.

Notice that even if Gehazi took only money and clothing from Naaman, Elisha in the above verse mentions so many other things, including servants. He is trying to make a point that Gehazi could have acquired much more in God's plan than he managed through his craft.

I believe that before God entrusts someone with the deeper wealth of His wisdom and anointing, that person must first demonstrate his preference for that anointing over worldly affluence. Not everybody does.

When you read that story, it's easy to marvel at how foolish Gehazi was. But faced with a similar situation, some ministers of God today have comfortably taken the path of Gehazi and wound up with leprosy.

Their leprosy does not manifest in the form of a sore body like it did then. It is marked by a lost anointing, curtailed effectiveness, deep regret and a lifetime of wondering what could have been.

Some leprous ministers continue to survive on reputation, holding onto their glorious past to mask the reality of their empty present, just like Gehazi who was last recorded telling a curious king all the stories of Elisha's exploits.

Selling discontent

There's a dear friend of mine, a preacher of renown in my country, such an anointed and erudite speaker, a man from whom I have learnt many things. I have not met anybody so immaculate in his approach, a stickler on class and etiquette who frowns on any form of disorder. He does have an eye for elegance, a fact that is apparent from his dress sense, choice of paintings and antique pieces that hang in his house.

This gentleman speaks to large audiences mostly across the border in Kenya. In spite of his proclivity to the finer things in life, he is a man who contentedly lives within his measure of faith. I noticed that he tends to keep away from the company of some fellow preachers.

I often wondered why.

One day as we had a cup of coffee he mentioned casually that he got wary of running into preachers who subtly suggest that with the sort of audiences he routinely commands, and the authority he wields, he should be living a more opulent life.

That's the other thing about mammon. Most of his converts are not content sticking to their acquisitive ways; they usually become involuntary evangelists of mammon, trying to win over as many people as possible. Their messages are often subtle and inadvertent but pernicious nonetheless. What's in their hearts often comes out one way or another and it does have an enticing edge to it because it takes the insidiousness out of their weakness and attempts to put a positive spin to it.

They use phrases like 'make the most of your position' to plant seeds of discontent among people who are pursuing God's plan.

Paul says that *"now godliness with contentment is great gain."* (1 Tim 6:6)

That's because discontentment is a very easy commodity to sell. That's why it has been a choice weapon of the devil in all generations of humanity, starting from Eve, who in spite of living in literal paradise in the Garden of Eden, easily bought into the idea that there must be something more exciting than what she already had.

Discontent easily destroys marriages, workplace environments, companies, churches and every form of order. It takes time and effort to build harmony but disgruntlement spreads like a wild fire and easily dismantles what has been painstakingly built.

Think about the children of Israel who saw the Red Sea parted for them to walk through and saw the corpses of the

Egyptian army by the seashore. *"Thus Israel saw the great work which the Lord had done in Egypt, so the people feared the Lord, and believed the Lord and His servant Moses."* (Ex 14: 31).

But all it took was a month and a half and the same congregation said: *"Oh that we had died by the hand of the Lord in Egypt, when we sat by the pots of meat and when we ate bread to the full."* (Ex 16:3)

They initially welcomed the manna gladly and rejoiced over it. But the mixed generation easily sold discontentment and made Israel despise the bread from heaven.

"We remember the fish we ate freely in Egypt, the cucumbers, the melons, the leeks, the onions, and the garlic; but now our whole being is dried up; there is nothing at all except this manna before our eyes." (Num 11: 5-6)

It's so easy to buy into discontentment.

Think about how much easier it was for the ten spies to spread their message of doom and gloom to the congregation of Israel in Numbers 13 than it was for Joshua and Caleb to preach faith and positivity.

That's why Paul tells Timothy: *"From such withdraw yourself."* (1 Timothy 6:5)

He is talking about evangelists of mammon, whom he calls "men of corrupt minds... who suppose that godliness is a means of (financial) gain".

Their message is so alluring in that it builds an unhealthy sense of urgency and presents enticing shortcuts to prosperity in these last days when the good old virtue that is patience is in short supply. And the Apostle Paul warned about these days in regard to greed when he wrote that:

"But understand this, that in the last days will come (set in) perilous times of great stress and trouble [hard to deal with and hard to bear]. For people will be lovers of self and [utterly] self-centered, **lovers of money and aroused by an inordinate [greedy] desire for wealth**......." (2Tim 3:1-2)

The more you listen to these evangelists of mammon who are skilled at selling discontentment the more you start feeling like the world is passing you by. The shortcuts they present will ALWAYS involve sacrificing of principles or values in haste for wealth. Those who make the first step will find it a lot easier to make consequent steps.

Whatever your calling, if you stick to God's plan it will always lead to prosperity. Poverty and need are not His intended destination for anyone.

David was anointed to become king of Israel in his teenage, but didn't sit on any throne until thirteen years later, and had to wait for another seven years to become king of the whole nation. Like everybody else he had to wait patiently for God's promise and those years of training often present many temptations to give up, to lose faith, to make things happen in your own way and, especially, to take a shortcut to wealth. He describes the allure of mammon in the 73rd Psalm.

"But as for me, my feet had almost stumbled; my steps nearly slipped. For I was envious of the boastful, when I saw the prosperity of the wicked.....Their eyes bulge with abundance; they have more than heart could wish. They scoff and... speak loftily."

It's a snare to even behold the ways of people who prosper through craft. They often seem to have it all their way. Even if their hearts are pierced throw with many sorrows as Paul says (1 Timothy 6:10), that is not apparent to the outside observer. What is evident is the opulence, the comfort, the luxury and the scoffing (at those who will not go down that path).

They speak loftily and present a rosy picture of their life even if deep down most of them — like Gehazi who spoke fondly of his days under Elisha — wish they had kept on the straight path. It's a sad thing for Gehazi to look at his leprous skin and silently wish he could return to the days of his innocence when he faithfully served the man of God.

Is there a way back for people who let mammon corrupt their innocence?

Of course there is.

Jesus' prescribed remedy

Unfortunately, people who have been afflicted with the rich man virus often find themselves in a position of helpless inactivity. They know where they ought to be. They know what they must do to get there. In most cases, however, their resolve has been weakened by the comforts of wealth. It's natural that someone who has been soaked in the rain, having come into the house and warmed up, is more reluctant to step back into the downpour than one who hasn't been there at all.

That's why God prefers that all the lessons of the wilderness are learnt while still in the wilderness. The book of Deuteronomy explains why God lets Israel go through the wilderness.

*"...to humble you and test you, to know what was in your heart, so He humbled you, allowed you to hunger, and fed you with manna, that He might test you, **to do you good in the end.**"* (Deut 8:2, 3, 15, 16).

It's never a good thing when people who took a shortcut into the Promised Land, and have tasted the good thereof, have drunk from the brooks of water, from the fountains and springs that flow out of valleys and hills, have eaten of the wheat and the barley, drunk of the vines, fig trees, pomegranates, oil and honey; it's never a pleasant experience when such people find that they must go back into the wilderness to attend classes they skipped.

Sadly, that's the remedy for people who allowed the love of money to short-circuit their development process and *"strayed from the faith in their greediness and pierced themselves through with many sorrows"* (1 Timothy 6:10).

I will refer back to a text from the Bible that I have already used a number of times. When the rich ruler came to Jesus in Luke 18, he expected to hear something new. I can imagine the look of accomplishment on his face when he said "all these things I have kept from my youth".

"So when Jesus heard these things, He said to him, "You still lack one thing. Sell all that you have and distribute to the poor, and you will have treasure in heaven; and come, follow Me."

But when he heard this, he became very sorrowful, for he was very rich.

Jesus knew that in spite of his piety he had another god sitting on the throne of his heart. And he could only get the joy of salvation when that god was dethroned. But he had a deep attachment to his wealth and wasn't quite ready to surrender it.

Christians who allowed mammon to creep into their lives and are consequently driven by greed often have to go back several steps and start over. Sometimes, depending on how much the virus has eaten at their hearts, the only way they can lose attachment to their wealth is by losing the wealth altogether. The rich ruler had sunk that low.

It's a very unfortunate stage for anyone to get to. Even more unfortunate is the fact that many people confronted with the choice between their wealth and God's way will opt for their wealth and walk away miserable like the rich ruler.

The process of going back into the wilderness to learn lessons that were skipped has to be voluntary. God will not force it on anyone. When King David was confronted by the prophet Nathan, he humbly accepted God's judgment and took it manfully. Because he had misused his authority to overthrow justice, he had to lose the throne for a while and be on the run all over again at a time of his life when he thought such things belonged in his turbulent past.

Imagine how much more difficult it was for David to flee into the mountains after he had tasted the joys of the palace. But he went through it, was fully restored, and God made his name great.

How many leaders or ministers have lost the anointing or the joy of their salvation as David says, or even their ministries because they succumbed to the allure of power, wealth and societal position? Having received all those things, they soon realize that it was never worth it without God.

Many of them get stuck in between two worlds; too enlightened to completely enjoy the best of Babylon and yet too cowardly to embark on what seems like an arduous journey back into God's plan for their lives. Most of them remain in that state of paralysis.

All they have to do is surrender.

It's not easy. But it's worth it.

After a little pain and deprivation, God will gladly restore them. When the wilderness syllabus is fully covered, they will return into the land of abundance, of figs and pomegranates, and they will never have to leave it again. God will restore the glory that departed from their lives the day they chose the gold. And the gold will be restored too.

It's a matter of personal conviction. Only the inner witness can prescribe remedy for each specific case.

Ironically, those who, on reading this, get on the defensive and assert that they haven't been infected by the rich man virus are more likely to be suffering from it. And then those who admit to suffering from it but immediately cling to the belief that they haven't gotten to the stage where they must surrender their wealth have probably gotten to that stage.

It's my hope, however, that a majority of the people reading this text will find it useful for preventive rather than curative reasons.

~ End ~